TUESDAY

IS

CHICKEN

and Turkey and Chicken Soup and Chicken Salads and More

TIME LIFE
CUSTOM
PUBLISHING

TIME-LIFE BOOKS, ALEXANDRIA, VIRGINIA

TIME-LIFE BOOKS IS A DIVISION OF TIME LIFE INC.

PRESIDENT and CEO, Time Life Inc.	John M. Fahey Jr.
PRESIDENT, Time-Life Books	John D. Hall

TIME-LIFE CUSTOM PUBLISHING

VICE PRESIDENT and PUBLISHER	Terry Newell
Director of Sales	Neil Levin
Director of New Product Development	Regina Hall
Managing Editor	Donia Ann Steele
Editorial Director	Jennifer Pearce
Senior Art Director	Christopher M. Register
Director of Financial Operations	J. Brian Birky
Financial Analyst	Trish Palini
Sales Manager	Liz Ziehl
Retail Promotions Manager	Gary Stoiber
Associate Marketing Manager	Dana A. Coleman
Retail Operations Manager	Valerie Lewis
Production Manager	Carolyn Bounds
Quality Assurance Manager	James D. King
Executive Assistant	Tammy York

Illustrations: William Neeper

Produced by Rebus, Inc.
New York, New York

Library of Congress Cataloging-in-Publication Data
Tuesday is chicken and turkey and chicken soup and chicken salads and more.
p. cm. -- (The everyday cookbooks)
Includes index.
ISBN 0-8094-9187-7
1. Cookery (Poultry) I. Time-Life Books. II. Series.
TX750.T84 1995
641.6'65--dc20   95-10415
                                                        CIP

Introduction

Remember when you could tell what day of the week it was by what Mom was making for dinner? It was predictable, and comforting, and—as far as Mom was concerned—efficient. But every now and then, didn't you wish she would give her usual chicken recipe a rest and try something new? Now here's a cookbook that not only helps you plan meals like Mom used to make but gives you a wonderful variety of recipes, too. With *Tuesday Is Chicken,* you can offer your family a delightfully different chicken meal every week.

To make life even easier, this cookbook includes the following features:

- There are no difficult techniques or exotic ingredients. All of the recipes can be made with supermarket-available foods and a great many of them can be made entirely with ingredients already in the pantry.

- Each recipe is designed with everyone's busy schedule in mind, with most taking under 30 minutes to prepare. These recipes are labeled "Extra-Quick" and are marked with this symbol: ◆ (A full listing of the extra-quick recipes is included in the index under the heading Extra-Quick.)

- Many of the recipes include lower-fat alternatives, such as reduced-fat sour cream and low-fat milk. In addition, we have created a number of recipes that get fewer than 30 percent of their calories from fat. These recipes are labeled "Low-Fat" and are marked with this symbol: ◇ (A full listing of the low-fat recipes is included in the index under the heading Low-Fat.)

- As a further help to the cook, there are notes throughout the book that provide simple variations on recipes, cooking shortcuts or tips on how to lower fat, suggestions for simple desserts that can be made for weekday meals, and substitutions, in case you can't find (or don't like) certain ingredients.

- In a special section called "Family Favorites," we include recipes that even the pickiest eaters will like, such as Chicken and Mixed Vegetable Grill and Turkey Fricassee with Egg Noodles.

But best of all, in *Tuesday Is Chicken* there are enough delicious poultry recipes for more than two years' worth of Tuesdays!

CONTENTS

GRILLS AND BROILS

SALADS

FAMILY FAVORITES

INDEX

HOT-AND-SOUR CHICKEN SOUP

SERVES 4

◆ EXTRA-QUICK ◇ LOW-FAT

3 CUPS CHICKEN BROTH, PREFERABLY
    REDUCED-SODIUM

¼ POUND SMALL MUSHROOMS

½ CUP CANNED SLICED BAMBOO
    SHOOTS

3 QUARTER-SIZE SLICES FRESH GINGER,
    UNPEELED

2 GARLIC CLOVES, MINCED

2 TEASPOONS REDUCED-SODIUM SOY
    SAUCE

¼ TEASPOON RED PEPPER FLAKES

1 POUND SKINLESS, BONELESS CHICKEN
    BREASTS

1 TABLESPOON ORIENTAL (DARK)
    SESAME OIL

3 TABLESPOONS RED WINE VINEGAR
    OR CIDER VINEGAR

2 TABLESPOONS CORNSTARCH

1 EGG

2 SCALLIONS, FINELY CHOPPED

¼ CUP (PACKED) CILANTRO SPRIGS,
    FINELY CHOPPED

1. In a medium saucepan, bring the broth, ½ cup of water, the mushrooms, bamboo shoots, ginger, garlic, soy sauce, and red pepper flakes to a boil over medium-high heat. Reduce the heat to low, cover, and simmer while you prepare the remaining ingredients.

2. Cut the chicken across the grain into ¼-inch slices. In a medium bowl, combine the chicken slices and the sesame oil, and toss to blend.

3. In a small bowl, combine the vinegar and cornstarch, and stir to blend. In another small bowl, lightly beat the egg.

4. Increase the heat under the broth to medium-high and return it to a boil. Add the chicken slices. Stirring constantly, gradually pour in the beaten egg. Stir in the vinegar mixture. Cook, stirring occasionally, until the chicken is cooked through and the soup is slightly thickened, about 3 minutes.

5. Stir in the scallions. Serve the soup sprinkled with the cilantro. If desired, remove the ginger slices before serving.

Chicken-Noodle Soup with Spinach

SERVES 4

◆ EXTRA-QUICK ◇ LOW-FAT

3 CUPS CHICKEN BROTH
1 TEASPOON THYME
¼ TEASPOON BLACK PEPPER
1¼ POUNDS BONE-IN CHICKEN THIGHS
2 MEDIUM CARROTS, THINLY SLICED
1 CUP EGG NOODLES

2 CUPS (PACKED) FRESH SPINACH
   LEAVES, TORN INTO BITE-SIZE
   PIECES, OR ½ CUP FROZEN CHOPPED
   SPINACH, THAWED
1 CUP FROZEN CORN

1. In a large saucepan, bring the broth, 2 cups of water, the thyme, and pepper to a boil over high heat. Add the chicken and return the liquid to a boil. Reduce the heat to medium-low, cover, and simmer for 10 minutes. Transfer the chicken to a plate to cool.

2. Return the broth to a boil over medium-high heat. Add the carrots and noodles, and cook until the noodles are al dente according to package directions.

3. Meanwhile, remove the skin and bones from the chicken and discard. Cut the meat into bite-size pieces (it will still be slightly pink).

4. Return the chicken to the soup. Add the spinach and corn, reduce the heat to medium, and cook until the chicken is cooked through, about 3 minutes.

5. Ladle the soup into 4 bowls and serve hot.

Chicken Tortilla Soup

SERVES 4

1 MEDIUM ONION, COARSELY CHOPPED
3 GARLIC CLOVES, MINCED
⅓ CUP (PACKED) FINELY CHOPPED
    CILANTRO
1 TABLESPOON PLUS 2 TEASPOONS OIL
2 TEASPOONS CUMIN
1½ TEASPOONS OREGANO
½ TEASPOON BLACK PEPPER
½ POUND SKINLESS, BONELESS
    CHICKEN BREASTS
2 CUPS CHICKEN BROTH

ONE 14½-OUNCE CAN NO-SALT-ADDED
    STEWED TOMATOES
1 CUP TOMATO JUICE
2 TEASPOONS GRATED LIME ZEST
2 TABLESPOONS FRESH LIME JUICE
½ TEASPOON WORCESTERSHIRE SAUCE
4 SMALL CORN TORTILLAS
1 FRESH OR PICKLED JALAPEÑO PEPPER,
    SEEDED AND MINCED
½ CUP SHREDDED MONTEREY JACK
    CHEESE

1. Preheat the broiler.

2. In a small bowl, combine half the onion, half the garlic, and half the cilantro. Stir in 1 tablespoon of the oil, 1 teaspoon of the cumin, ½ teaspoon of the oregano, and ¼ teaspoon of the black pepper.

3. Place the chicken on a broiler pan and spoon the onion-herb mixture on top. Broil 4 inches from the heat for 7 minutes. Turn the chicken over, baste with any pan juices, and broil for 7 minutes longer, or until cooked through. Transfer the chicken to a plate to cool. Preheat the oven to 400°.

4. Meanwhile, in a medium saucepan, warm the remaining 2 teaspoons oil over medium-high heat. Add the remaining onion and garlic, and stir-fry until the onion begins to brown, 3 to 4 minutes.

5. Add the broth, 1 cup of water, the tomatoes, tomato juice, lime zest, lime juice, Worcestershire sauce, and the remaining cilantro, 1 teaspoon cumin, 1 teaspoon oregano, and ¼ teaspoon black pepper. Bring the mixture to a boil; reduce the heat to low, cover, and simmer while you prepare the tortillas.

6. Cut each tortilla in half, then cut each half crosswise into strips. Place on a baking sheet and bake for 7 minutes, or until toasted. Pull the cooled chicken apart into shreds.

7. Stir the jalapeño into the simmering soup. Ladle the soup into 4 bowls and top with the chicken, tortilla strips, and cheese.

Chunky Chicken-Potato Soup

SERVES 4

◆ EXTRA-QUICK

4 TABLESPOONS UNSALTED BUTTER

1 MEDIUM ONION, COARSELY CHOPPED

¼ CUP FLOUR

4½ CUPS CHICKEN BROTH, PREFERABLY
REDUCED-SODIUM

2 MEDIUM ALL-PURPOSE POTATOES
(ABOUT 1 POUND), PEELED AND CUT
INTO ½-INCH CUBES

¼ TEASPOON BLACK PEPPER

1½ CUPS LOW-FAT MILK

1½ CUPS CUBED COOKED CHICKEN
(ABOUT ½ POUND)

1 CUP SMALL BROCCOLI FLORETS

ONE 16-OUNCE CAN CORN, DRAINED

1. In a large saucepan, melt the butter over medium heat. Add the onion and cook, stirring frequently, until wilted, about 2 minutes.

2. Stir in the flour and cook, stirring constantly, until the flour and butter are completely blended, about 1 minute.

3. Gradually pour in the broth, stirring constantly, and return the mixture to a boil. Stir in the potatoes and pepper. Reduce the heat

to medium-low, cover, and simmer, stirring occasionally, until the potatoes are tender, about 15 minutes.

4. Increase the heat to medium and return the mixture to a boil. Stir in the milk, chicken, broccoli, and corn. Cook until the broccoli is crisp-tender and the chicken is heated through, 2 to 3 minutes longer.

5. Ladle the soup into 4 bowls and serve hot.

KITCHEN NOTE: *Making soup is one of the best ways to use leftovers, since exact quantities are not critical to the soup's success. This recipe calls for about half a pound of leftover chicken, but a little bit more or less won't do any harm. And if you don't have broccoli on hand, you can omit it or replace it with cauliflower (add it when you put in the potatoes) or sliced mushrooms (add them at the end with the chicken).*

CHEDDAR-CHICKEN CHOWDER

SERVES 4

◆ EXTRA-QUICK

4 TABLESPOONS UNSALTED BUTTER

4 SCALLIONS, COARSELY CHOPPED

1 SMALL GARLIC CLOVE, MINCED

⅓ CUP FLOUR

2 CUPS CHICKEN BROTH

1½ TEASPOONS THYME

¼ TEASPOON BLACK PEPPER

2 MEDIUM CARROTS, ROUGHLY DICED

2 MEDIUM CELERY RIBS, ROUGHLY DICED

1 POUND SKINLESS, BONELESS CHICKEN BREASTS, CUT INTO ½-INCH CHUNKS

1 CUP LOW-FAT MILK

1 CUP GRATED WHITE OR YELLOW CHEDDAR CHEESE

1. In a large saucepan, warm the butter over medium-high heat until melted. Add the scallions and garlic, and cook until the scallions are softened, about 3 minutes.

2. Reduce the heat to medium, stir in the flour, and cook, stirring constantly, until it is no longer visible, about 30 seconds.

3. Increase the heat to medium-high and stir in the broth, 1 cup of water, thyme, and pepper. Bring the mixture to a boil. Reduce the heat to low, cover, and simmer for 5 minutes.

4. Uncover the broth and return it to a boil over medium-high heat. Add the carrots, celery, and chicken, and cook, stirring occasionally, until the chicken is cooked through, about 6 minutes.

5. Stir in the milk and cheese, and cook, stirring frequently, until the cheese is melted, about 5 minutes. Ladle the chowder into 4 bowls and serve hot.

TURKEY GOULASH SOUP

SERVES 6

◇ LOW-FAT

2 TEASPOONS OLIVE OIL

3 MEDIUM ONIONS, THINLY SLICED

2 MEDIUM GREEN BELL PEPPERS, CUT INTO ¾-INCH SQUARES

2 TABLESPOONS PAPRIKA, PREFERABLY HUNGARIAN

¼ TEASPOON CUMIN

¼ TEASPOON BLACK PEPPER

8 CUPS CHICKEN BROTH, PREFERABLY REDUCED-SODIUM

2 TABLESPOONS CORNSTARCH

¼ POUND WIDE EGG NOODLES

1 POUND TURKEY CUTLETS, SLICED ACROSS THE GRAIN INTO THIN STRIPS

¼ TEASPOON SALT

1. In a large pot, warm the oil over medium heat. Add the onions and cook, stirring frequently, until browned, about 15 minutes.

2. Stir in the bell peppers, paprika, cumin, black pepper, and all but ¼ cup of the broth. In a cup, combine the cornstarch and the reserved ¼ cup broth, stir to blend, and stir into the pot. Bring the mixture to a simmer and cook, partially covered, for 20 minutes.

3. Meanwhile, in another large pot of boiling water, cook the noodles until al dente according to package directions. Drain the noodles, rinse them under cold running water, and set aside.

4. Add the turkey strips to the simmering broth and poach them until they are opaque, 3 to 4 minutes. Stir in the noodles and salt. Cook the soup for 2 minutes more, ladle into 6 bowls, and serve hot.

SWEET AFTERTHOUGHT: *For a dessert with a Hungarian theme, try this simple sundae. In a small saucepan, heat canned cherries (with their syrup) or canned apricots cut into quarters (also with their syrup). When hot, stir in 2 or 3 teaspoons of butter and a teaspoon or so of cherry or apricot brandy. Remove from the heat and serve warm over ice cream or frozen yogurt.*

Make-Ahead Turkey Newburg

SERVES 6

1 CUP CHICKEN BROTH, PREFERABLY
   REDUCED-SODIUM
½ CUP DRY SHERRY
3 TABLESPOONS FLOUR
1 TEASPOON BROWN SUGAR
1¾ POUNDS SKINLESS, BONELESS
   TURKEY BREAST, CUT INTO
   1-INCH CHUNKS

½ POUND HAM, UNSLICED, CUT INTO
   THICK MATCHSTICKS
2 TABLESPOONS OLIVE OIL
1½ TEASPOONS ROSEMARY, CRUMBLED
¼ TEASPOON BLACK PEPPER
1 TABLESPOON UNSALTED BUTTER
1 POUND SMALL MUSHROOMS

1. In a small bowl or screw-top jar, combine the broth, 6 tablespoons of the sherry, the flour, and ½ teaspoon of the brown sugar. Stir or shake to blend well. Cover and refrigerate until ready to cook the dish.

2. In a medium bowl, combine the turkey, ham, the remaining 2 tablespoons sherry, the remaining ½ teaspoon sugar, 1 tablespoon of the oil, the rosemary, and pepper. Toss to coat well, cover, and refrigerate, stirring occasionally, for at least 30 minutes or up to 1 day.

3. In a large skillet, warm the remaining 1 tablespoon oil with the butter over medium-high heat until the butter is melted. Add the mushrooms and cook, stirring frequently, until they begin to wilt, about 5 minutes.

4. Add the turkey-ham mixture (including the marinade) and cook, stirring frequently, until the turkey is nearly cooked through, 8 to 10 minutes.

5. Stir or shake the broth mixture to recombine and add it to the skillet. Bring the mixture to a boil and cook, stirring constantly, until the sauce has thickened and the turkey is cooked through, 2 to 3 minutes. Spoon into 6 serving bowls and serve hot.

KITCHEN NOTE: *All of the components for this rich-tasting stew can be prepared ahead so that the dish needs only 30 minutes of assembly—about the time it takes to cook rice or noodles to go with it. Shaking the sauce ingredients in a jar to combine them is a useful trick: Try it the next time you need to blend flour and liquid for making gravy.*

TURKEY COUNTRY CAPTAIN

SERVES 4

1½ TABLESPOONS OLIVE OIL

1½ TABLESPOONS UNSALTED BUTTER

1½ POUNDS SKINLESS, BONELESS
TURKEY BREAST, CUT INTO
¾-INCH CUBES

1 MEDIUM ONION, THINLY SLICED

1 GARLIC CLOVE, MINCED

1 TABLESPOON FLOUR

1 TABLESPOON CURRY POWDER

½ TEASPOON SALT

½ TEASPOON THYME

¼ TEASPOON CINNAMON

¼ TEASPOON GROUND CLOVES

PINCH OF CAYENNE PEPPER

¾ CUP DRY WHITE WINE

4 MEDIUM TOMATOES, SEEDED AND
COARSELY CHOPPED

1 MEDIUM RED BELL PEPPER, CUT INTO
THIN STRIPS

1 MEDIUM GREEN BELL PEPPER, CUT
INTO THIN STRIPS

½ CUP RAISINS

½ CUP CHOPPED PARSLEY

½ CUP WHOLE ALMONDS, TOASTED

1. In a large skillet, warm the oil with the butter over medium-high heat until the butter is melted. Add the turkey, onion, and garlic, and cook, stirring occasionally, until the turkey is lightly browned, 8 to 10 minutes.

2. Add the flour, curry powder, salt, thyme, cinnamon, cloves, and cayenne, and stir to coat the turkey. Stir in the wine, tomatoes, and bell peppers. Cover, reduce the heat to medium-low, and simmer until the turkey is tender, 20 to 25 minutes.

3. Add the raisins and ¼ cup of the parsley and simmer for 5 minutes.

4. Serve the stew sprinkled with the almonds and the remaining ¼ cup parsley.

Chicken Stew with Zucchini and Tomatoes

SERVES 4

◇ LOW-FAT

2½ POUNDS TOMATOES, COARSELY
   CHOPPED, OR ONE 28-OUNCE CAN
   NO-SALT-ADDED WHOLE TOMATOES,
   COARSELY CHOPPED
1½ CUPS CHICKEN BROTH, PREFERABLY
   REDUCED-SODIUM
2 GARLIC CLOVES, MINCED
1 TEASPOON BASIL
1 TEASPOON SUGAR

½ TO ¾ TEASPOON CHILI POWDER
½ TEASPOON SALT
¼ TEASPOON BLACK PEPPER
2 BONE-IN CHICKEN BREAST HALVES,
   SKINNED
¼ POUND WIDE EGG NOODLES
2 MEDIUM ZUCCHINI, CUT INTO
   THIN ROUNDS

1. In a large saucepan, combine the tomatoes, broth, garlic, basil, sugar, chili powder, salt, and pepper. Bring to a simmer over medium heat and cook, stirring occasionally, for 10 minutes.

2. Add the chicken, reduce the heat to low, and poach for 12 minutes—it will still be slightly undercooked. With a slotted spoon, transfer the chicken to a cutting board. Remove the bones from the chicken and discard. Cut the meat into bite-size pieces.

3. Meanwhile, in a large pot of boiling water, cook the noodles for 3 minutes—they will still be undercooked.

4. Drain the noodles well, then add them to the stew. Stir in the zucchini and the chicken pieces. Continue cooking until the noodles are tender and the chicken is cooked through, about 5 minutes. Serve hot.

NEW ORLEANS-STYLE CHICKEN STEW

SERVES 4

¼ CUP FLOUR

1 TEASPOON THYME

⅛ TEASPOON CAYENNE PEPPER

1¼ POUNDS SKINLESS, BONELESS
   CHICKEN BREASTS, CUT INTO PIECES

1 TABLESPOON VEGETABLE OIL

2 TABLESPOONS UNSALTED BUTTER

3 GARLIC CLOVES, MINCED

ONE 14½-OUNCE CAN STEWED
   TOMATOES

¼ CUP CHICKEN BROTH

8 SCALLIONS, COARSELY CHOPPED

2 CELERY RIBS, DICED

1 LARGE RED BELL PEPPER, DICED

3 DROPS HOT PEPPER SAUCE

1 BAY LEAF

¼ POUND KIELBASA OR OTHER
   PRECOOKED GARLIC SAUSAGE, DICED

1. In a small plastic bag, combine the flour, thyme, and cayenne, and shake to mix. Add the chicken and shake to coat lightly. Reserve the excess seasoned flour.

2. In a large skillet, warm the oil with 1 tablespoon of the butter over medium-high heat until the butter is melted. Add the chicken and cook, stirring frequently, until well browned all over, about 7 minutes. With a slotted spoon, transfer the chicken to a plate and cover loosely with foil to keep warm.

3. Add the remaining 1 tablespoon butter to the skillet and heat until melted. Add the garlic. Stir in the reserved flour mixture and cook, stirring constantly, until the flour is no longer visible, about 1 minute.

4. Stir in the tomatoes, broth, scallions, celery, bell pepper, hot pepper sauce, and bay leaf; break up the tomatoes with the back of a spoon. Bring the mixture to a boil over medium-high heat. Reduce the heat to low, cover, and simmer, stirring occasionally, until the vegetables are tender, about 15 minutes.

5. Return the stew to a boil over medium-high heat. Return the chicken (and any juices that have collected on the plate) to the skillet. Stir in the sausage and cook until the chicken is cooked through, about 3 minutes. Remove and discard the bay leaf from the stew. Divide the stew among 4 bowls and serve hot.

Spicy White Bean Turkey Stew

SERVES 4

◇ LOW-FAT

1 TABLESPOON OLIVE OIL

8 SCALLIONS, COARSELY CHOPPED

3 GARLIC CLOVES, MINCED

½ POUND TURKEY CUTLETS, CUT INTO
   BITE-SIZE PIECES

1 TEASPOON CUMIN

½ TEASPOON GROUND GINGER

¼ TEASPOON BLACK PEPPER

¼ TEASPOON RED PEPPER FLAKES

PINCH OF CAYENNE PEPPER

ONE 14½-OUNCE CAN NO-SALT-ADDED
   WHOLE TOMATOES

1 LARGE GREEN BELL PEPPER, CUT INTO
   BITE-SIZE PIECES

1 LARGE RED BELL PEPPER, CUT INTO
   BITE-SIZE PIECES

½ CUP CHICKEN BROTH

ONE 20-OUNCE CAN WHITE KIDNEY
   BEANS (CANNELLINI), RINSED AND
   DRAINED

1. In a large nonstick skillet, warm the oil over medium-high heat. Add the scallions and garlic, and cook, stirring frequently, until they begin to brown, 2 to 3 minutes.

2. Add the turkey and cook, stirring frequently, until the turkey is no longer pink, 4 to 5 minutes.

3. Add the cumin, ginger, black pepper, red pepper flakes, and cayenne, and stir-fry until the spices are fragrant, about 30 seconds. Add the tomatoes, bell peppers, and broth. Bring the mixture to a boil over medium-high heat,

breaking up the tomatoes with the back of a spoon. Reduce the heat to low, cover, and simmer for 15 minutes.

4. Meanwhile, place 1 cup of the beans in a bowl and, with a fork or potato masher, mash them to a coarse purée.

5. Increase the heat under the skillet to medium-high and stir in the whole beans and the bean purée. Cook uncovered, stirring frequently, until the beans are heated through, about 5 minutes. Spoon the turkey stew into 4 bowls and serve hot.

CHICKEN AND TINY STAR PASTA STEW

SERVES 4

◆ EXTRA-QUICK

2 TABLESPOONS BUTTER

3 TABLESPOONS FLOUR

3 CUPS CHICKEN BROTH, PREFERABLY
   REDUCED-SODIUM

¾ TEASPOON THYME

¼ TEASPOON BLACK PEPPER

2 LARGE CARROTS, VERY THINLY
   SLICED

½ CUP TINY PASTA STARS, OR OTHER
   SMALL PASTA SHAPE

1 POUND SKINLESS, BONELESS CHICKEN
   BREASTS, CUT INTO BITE-SIZE PIECES

¼ POUND MUSHROOMS, THINLY SLICED

10 CHERRY TOMATOES

6 SCALLIONS, COARSELY CHOPPED

1. In a large saucepan, melt the butter over medium heat. Stir in the flour and cook, stirring constantly, until the flour has completely absorbed the butter, about 1 minute.

2. Increase the heat to medium-high, gradually add a small amount of the broth, and stir to combine with the butter and flour. Add the remaining broth, the thyme, and pepper, and bring to a boil, stirring constantly, until the mixture is slightly thickened.

3. Add the carrots and pasta, and cook for 3 minutes.

4. Stir in the chicken, mushrooms, and whole tomatoes. Return the mixture to a boil, breaking up the tomatoes with the back of a spoon. Reduce the heat to medium-low, cover, and simmer until the chicken is cooked through, about 5 minutes.

5. Stir in the scallions, ladle the stew into 4 bowls, and serve hot.

SUBSTITUTION: *The miniature star pasta used here is sometimes labeled "stelline" or "pastina." You could also use alphabets, or orzo (pasta the size and shape of rice grains). In a pinch, break thin spaghetti into 1-inch lengths.*

Chicken Paprika with Ziti

SERVES 4

2 TABLESPOONS FLOUR
2 TABLESPOONS PAPRIKA
¾ TEASPOON SALT
¼ TEASPOON BLACK PEPPER
2 TABLESPOONS OLIVE OIL
2 TABLESPOONS UNSALTED BUTTER
4 SCALLIONS, COARSELY CHOPPED
3 GARLIC CLOVES, MINCED
1¼ POUNDS SKINLESS, BONELESS
  CHICKEN BREASTS, CUT ACROSS THE
  GRAIN INTO ¼-INCH-THICK SLICES

½ POUND ZITI
½ POUND SMALL MUSHROOMS, HALVED
½ CUP REDUCED-FAT SOUR CREAM
¼ CUP PLAIN LOW-FAT YOGURT
1 CUP COARSELY CHOPPED CANNED
  NO-SALT-ADDED WHOLE TOMATOES
½ CUP CHICKEN BROTH

1. In a medium bowl, combine the flour, paprika, salt, and pepper. Set aside.

2. In a large skillet, warm 1 tablespoon of the oil with 1 tablespoon of the butter over medium-high heat until the butter is melted. Add the scallions and garlic, and cook, stirring frequently, until the scallions are translucent, about 3 minutes.

3. Dredge the chicken in the seasoned flour mixture and reserve the excess. Add the chicken to the skillet and cook, stirring frequently, until cooked through, about 5 minutes. Transfer the chicken to a plate and set aside.

4. In a large pot of boiling water, cook the pasta until al dente according to package directions.

5. Meanwhile, add the remaining 1 tablespoon oil and 1 tablespoon butter to the skillet. Add the mushrooms and cook, stirring occasionally, for 5 minutes.

6. In a small bowl, combine the sour cream and yogurt. Stir in the reserved flour mixture.

7. Add the tomatoes to the skillet. Reduce the heat to medium and stir in the broth and sour cream mixture. Return the chicken to the skillet and cook, stirring occasionally, until heated through, about 2 minutes.

8. Drain the pasta, divide it among 4 plates, and spoon the sauce on top.

Indian-Style Tangy Turkey

SERVES 4

◇ LOW-FAT

¼ TEASPOON CINNAMON

1 CUP RICE

2 TABLESPOONS OLIVE OIL

1 MEDIUM ONION, THINLY SLICED

3 GARLIC CLOVES, MINCED

2 TEASPOONS CUMIN

1 TEASPOON GROUND GINGER

¼ TEASPOON NUTMEG

PINCH OF CAYENNE PEPPER

2 TABLESPOONS FLOUR

1 CUP CANNED STEWED TOMATOES

½ CUP CHICKEN BROTH

¼ TEASPOON SALT

¼ TEASPOON BLACK PEPPER

PINCH OF SUGAR

¼ CUP PLAIN LOW-FAT YOGURT

¼ CUP REDUCED-FAT SOUR CREAM

1 POUND TURKEY CUTLETS, CUT
  ACROSS THE GRAIN INTO
  ½-INCH-WIDE STRIPS

ONE 10-OUNCE PACKAGE FROZEN PEAS

¼ CUP CHOPPED CILANTRO

1. In a medium saucepan, bring 2 cups of water and the cinnamon to a boil over medium-high heat. Add the rice, reduce the heat to medium-low, cover, and simmer until the rice is tender, about 20 minutes.

2. Meanwhile, in a medium skillet, warm 1 tablespoon of the oil over medium-high heat. Add the onion and garlic, and cook, stirring frequently, until the mixture is light golden, 3 to 5 minutes.

3. Add the remaining 1 tablespoon oil, the cumin, ginger, nutmeg, and cayenne, and cook, stirring constantly, until the spices are fragrant, about 30 seconds. Blend in the flour and cook, stirring constantly, for 30 seconds.

4. Add the tomatoes, broth, salt, black pepper, and sugar. Bring the mixture to a boil, stirring, and cook until the sauce is slightly thickened, about 3 minutes. Reduce the heat to low, cover, and simmer for 3 minutes.

5. Meanwhile, in a small serving bowl, combine the yogurt and sour cream. Stir to blend.

6. Uncover the skillet, increase the heat to medium-high, and bring to a boil. Add the turkey and peas, and cook, stirring frequently, until the peas are hot and the turkey is just cooked through, about 5 minutes.

7. Spoon the rice onto 4 plates. Top with the turkey mixture, sprinkle with the cilantro, and serve with the yogurt sauce.

TURKEY PORCUPINES

SERVES 4

4 SCALLIONS

3 GARLIC CLOVES

3 QUARTER-SIZE SLICES FRESH GINGER

¼ CUP (PACKED) CILANTRO SPRIGS

1 POUND GROUND TURKEY

¼ CUP RICE

1 EGG

½ TEASPOON SALT

¼ TEASPOON BLACK PEPPER

1 TABLESPOON OLIVE OIL

1 CUP CHICKEN BROTH, PREFERABLY
   REDUCED-SODIUM

½ CUP CANNED CRUSHED TOMATOES

1 TABLESPOON CORNSTARCH

1. In a food processor, process the scallions, garlic, ginger, and cilantro until finely chopped.

2. In a medium bowl, combine the turkey, rice, egg, salt, pepper, and half of the scallion mixture. Mix gently until well combined. Using about 2 tablespoons of the turkey mixture for each, form the mixture into balls.

3. In a large skillet, warm the oil over medium-high heat. Add the remaining scallion mixture and cook, stirring frequently, until the mixture begins to brown, about 3 minutes.

4. Add ¾ cup of the broth and the tomatoes and bring the mixture to a boil. Add the turkey balls and return to a boil. Reduce the heat to low, cover, and simmer, stirring occasionally, until the rice is cooked, about 20 minutes.

5. In a small bowl, combine the remaining ¼ cup broth with the cornstarch. Stir to blend.

6. Uncover the skillet and return the mixture to a boil over high heat. Add the broth-cornstarch mixture and cook, stirring constantly, until the sauce has thickened slightly, about 1 minute. Serve hot.

VARIATION: *For Italian-style porcupines, use fresh basil in place of the cilantro and 1 tablespoon grated Parmesan in place of the ginger. If desired, add about 1½ tablespoons very finely minced black olives to the ground turkey mixture.*

Mediterranean Chicken Breasts with Yellow Rice

SERVES 4

3 TABLESPOONS FLOUR

½ TEASPOON BLACK PEPPER

4 SKINLESS, BONELESS CHICKEN BREAST
   HALVES (ABOUT 1¼ POUNDS TOTAL)

2 TABLESPOONS OLIVE OIL

2 MEDIUM ONIONS, THINLY SLICED

5 GARLIC CLOVES, MINCED

1 LARGE GREEN BELL PEPPER, CHOPPED

¼ POUND KIELBASA, DICED

1 CUP RICE

2 CUPS CHICKEN BROTH

¼ CUP CHOPPED PIMIENTO

¼ TEASPOON TURMERIC OR SAFFRON

1 TABLESPOON UNSALTED BUTTER

5 PLUM TOMATOES, CHOPPED

1 CUP DRY WHITE WINE

¼ TEASPOON SUGAR

1 BAY LEAF

1. In a bowl, combine the flour and black pepper. Dredge the chicken lightly in the seasoned flour and reserve the excess.

2. In a large skillet, warm 2 teaspoons of the oil over medium-high heat. Add the onions and half of the garlic, and cook until the onions are golden, about 5 minutes. Add the bell pepper and cook for 3 minutes. Transfer the vegetables to a plate.

3. Add 1 tablespoon of the oil to the skillet. Add the chicken and cook until browned, about 3 minutes per side. Transfer to a plate.

4. In a medium saucepan, warm the remaining 1 teaspoon oil over medium-high heat. Add the kielbasa and cook, stirring, for 3 minutes. Add the remaining garlic and the rice

and cook, stirring, for 1 minute. Add 1½ cups of the broth, ½ cup of water, the pimiento, and turmeric. Bring to a boil, reduce the heat to medium-low, cover, and simmer until the rice is tender, about 20 minutes.

5. Return the vegetable mixture to the skillet. Add the butter. Sprinkle with 1 tablespoon of the reserved flour mixture and cook, stirring constantly, until the flour is no longer visible, about 30 seconds. Add the tomatoes, wine, remaining ½ cup broth, the sugar, and bay leaf, and bring the mixture to a boil.

6. Return the chicken to the skillet, reduce the heat to low, cover, and simmer until the chicken is cooked, about 15 minutes. Discard the bay leaf. Serve the chicken over the rice.

Curried Chicken and Peas

SERVES 4

◆ EXTRA-QUICK

3 TABLESPOONS CORNSTARCH

¼ TEASPOON SALT

¼ TEASPOON BLACK PEPPER

4 SKINLESS, BONELESS CHICKEN BREAST
   HALVES (ABOUT 1¼ POUNDS TOTAL)

3 TABLESPOONS OLIVE OIL

5 SCALLIONS, COARSELY CHOPPED

2 GARLIC CLOVES, MINCED

1¼ CUPS CHICKEN BROTH, PREFERABLY
   REDUCED-SODIUM

2 TABLESPOONS MILD CURRY POWDER

1 TEASPOON BASIL

½ CUP GOLDEN RAISINS (OPTIONAL)

1 CUP FROZEN PEAS

1. In a shallow bowl, combine the cornstarch, salt, and pepper. Dredge the chicken lightly in the seasoned cornstarch. Remove the chicken, reserving the excess cornstarch.

2. In a large skillet, warm 1 tablespoon of the oil over medium-high heat. Add the scallions and garlic, and cook, stirring frequently, until the scallions begin to wilt, about 2 minutes.

3. Add the remaining 2 tablespoons oil to the skillet. Add the chicken, and cook until golden all over, 2 to 3 minutes per side.

4. Stir the broth into the reserved cornstarch and add it to the skillet. Stir in the curry powder and basil. Add the raisins (if using). Bring the mixture to a boil, reduce the heat to medium-low, cover, and simmer until the sauce is slightly thickened, about 5 minutes.

5. Uncover the skillet and increase the heat to medium-high. Turn the chicken over, add the peas, and cook, stirring frequently, for 5 minutes longer. Serve hot.

Sweet Afterthought: *For an almost-crème brûlée, make storebought vanilla pudding with half-and-half instead of milk and divide among custard cups. When the pudding is set and chilled, top with a thin layer of granulated brown sugar and place under the broiler until the sugar topping is caramelized (watch carefully).*

Tomato-Tarragon Braised Chicken Breasts

SERVES 4

3 TABLESPOONS FLOUR
¼ TEASPOON BLACK PEPPER
4 BONE-IN CHICKEN BREAST HALVES
 (ABOUT 2½ POUNDS TOTAL)
1 TABLESPOON OLIVE OIL
8 MEDIUM SHALLOTS, PEELED, OR 1
 MEDIUM ONION, CUT INTO WEDGES

2 GARLIC CLOVES, MINCED
1 CUP CANNED CRUSHED TOMATOES
½ CUP CHICKEN BROTH
3 TABLESPOONS MINCED FRESH
 TARRAGON, OR 1 TEASPOON DRIED
1 TEASPOON LIGHT BROWN SUGAR

1. In a plastic or paper bag, combine the flour and pepper, and shake to mix. Add the chicken and shake to coat lightly. Remove the chicken and reserve the excess seasoned flour.

2. In a large skillet, warm the oil over medium-high heat. Add the chicken, skin-side down, and cook until golden brown, about 6 minutes. Turn the chicken over and cook for 3 minutes. Transfer the chicken to a plate and cover loosely with foil to keep warm.

3. Stir the reserved seasoned flour into the skillet until the flour is no longer visible. Add the shallots, garlic, tomatoes, broth, tarragon, and brown sugar. Bring the mixture to a boil over medium-high heat.

4. Return the chicken (and any juices that have collected on the plate) to the skillet. Reduce the heat to medium-low, cover, and simmer for 5 minutes.

5. Turn the chicken over, stir the sauce well, and simmer, covered, until the chicken is cooked through, 10 to 15 minutes. Serve hot.

Chicken Thighs in Piquant Sauce

SERVES 4

3 TABLESPOONS PAPRIKA

1½ TEASPOONS OREGANO

¼ TEASPOON BLACK PEPPER

PINCH OF CAYENNE PEPPER

8 BONE-IN CHICKEN THIGHS (ABOUT
2½ POUNDS TOTAL), SKINNED

1 TABLESPOON OLIVE OIL

1 MEDIUM ONION, COARSELY CHOPPED

2 GARLIC CLOVES, MINCED

2 TABLESPOONS FLOUR

½ CUP CHICKEN BROTH

¼ CUP RED WINE VINEGAR

2 TABLESPOONS TOMATO PASTE

½ TEASPOON SUGAR

½ TEASPOON SALT

1. In a small plastic or paper bag, combine the paprika, ¾ teaspoon of the oregano, the black pepper, and cayenne, and shake to mix. Add the chicken and shake to coat lightly.

2. In a large skillet, warm the oil over medium-high heat. Add the chicken and cook until just beginning to char slightly, about 4 minutes per side. Transfer the chicken to a plate and cover loosely with foil to keep warm.

3. Add the onion and garlic to the skillet and cook, stirring frequently, for 1 minute. Stir in the flour and cook, stirring constantly, until the flour is no longer visible, about 30 seconds. Stir in the broth, vinegar, tomato paste, sugar, salt, and remaining ¾ teaspoon oregano until thoroughly combined.

4. Bring the mixture to a boil. Return the chicken (and any juices that have collected on the plate) to the skillet and let the mixture return to a boil. Reduce the heat to low, cover, and simmer for 5 minutes.

5. Turn the chicken over and cook, covered, until the chicken is cooked through, about 6 minutes longer. Divide the chicken and sauce among 4 plates and serve hot.

CHICKEN THIGHS WITH LIME AND CURRY

SERVES 4

2 TABLESPOONS FLOUR

¼ TEASPOON BLACK PEPPER

8 BONE-IN CHICKEN THIGHS, SKINNED
(ABOUT 2½ POUNDS TOTAL)

1 TABLESPOON OLIVE OIL

1 TABLESPOON UNSALTED BUTTER

1 MEDIUM RED ONION, COARSELY
CHOPPED

2 GARLIC CLOVES, MINCED

½ CUP CHICKEN BROTH

1½ TEASPOONS CURRY POWDER

3 DROPS HOT PEPPER SAUCE

⅓ CUP REDUCED-FAT SOUR CREAM

¼ CUP (PACKED) CILANTRO SPRIGS,
CHOPPED

¼ CUP FRESH LIME JUICE

2 TEASPOONS GRATED LIME ZEST

1. In a plastic or paper bag, combine the flour and pepper, and shake to mix. Add the chicken and shake to coat lightly. Remove the chicken; reserve the excess seasoned flour.

2. In a large skillet, warm the oil with the butter over medium-high heat until the butter is melted. Add the chicken and cook until golden all over, about 4 minutes per side. Transfer the chicken to a plate and cover loosely with foil to keep warm.

3. Add the onion and garlic to the skillet and cook, stirring frequently, for 1 minute. Add the reserved flour mixture and cook, stirring constantly, until the flour is no longer visible, about 30 seconds. Stir in the broth, curry powder, and hot pepper sauce, and bring the mixture to a boil. Reduce the heat to low, cover, and simmer for 5 minutes.

4. Return the broth mixture to a boil over medium-high heat. Stir in the sour cream, 2 tablespoons of the cilantro, the lime juice, and lime zest. Return the chicken (and any juices that have collected on the plate) to the skillet. Return the mixture to a boil and cook, uncovered, until the chicken is cooked through, about 5 minutes.

5. Divide the chicken and sauce among 4 plates and sprinkle the remaining cilantro on top.

Italian-Style Skillet Chicken

SERVES 4

2 TABLESPOONS VEGETABLE OIL

1 MEDIUM RED ONION, HALVED AND THICKLY SLICED

2 GARLIC CLOVES, MINCED

2½ POUNDS CHICKEN PARTS

ONE 28-OUNCE CAN CRUSHED TOMATOES

2 TABLESPOONS TOMATO PASTE

1 TEASPOON OREGANO

¼ TEASPOON SALT

¼ TEASPOON BLACK PEPPER

1 MEDIUM ZUCCHINI, THINLY SLICED

1 MEDIUM YELLOW SQUASH, THINLY SLICED

¼ POUND MUSHROOMS, THINLY SLICED

1. In a large skillet or flameproof casserole, warm the oil over medium-high heat. Add the onion and garlic, and cook, stirring frequently, until the onion begins to wilt, 1 to 2 minutes. With a slotted spoon, transfer the mixture to a plate.

2. Add the chicken to the skillet and brown on all sides, about 10 minutes.

3. Return the onion mixture to the skillet. Add the tomatoes, tomato paste, oregano, salt, and pepper. Bring the mixture to a boil, reduce the heat to medium-low, cover, and simmer for 30 minutes.

4. Stir in the zucchini, yellow squash, and mushrooms, and cook, uncovered, until the squashes are crisp-tender, about 10 minutes. Serve hot.

KITCHEN NOTE: *Cooking this dish in a microwave cuts about 20 minutes off the cooking time and lowers the fat levels because it omits the oil: In a 4-quart microwave-safe casserole, arrange the chicken with the thicker portions toward the rim of the dish. Sprinkle the onion on top. Omit the oil. Cover and cook at High for 10 minutes, turning the chicken over once. Stir in the remaining ingredients, re-cover and cook at High for 15 to 20 minutes or until the vegetables are tender and the chicken is cooked through.*

CHICKEN THIGHS CREOLE WITH ALMOND-ONION PILAF

SERVES 4

¼ CUP FLOUR

2 TEASPOONS PAPRIKA

½ TEASPOON SALT

¼ TEASPOON BLACK PEPPER

PINCH OF CAYENNE PEPPER

8 BONE-IN CHICKEN THIGHS (ABOUT
2½ POUNDS TOTAL)

2 TABLESPOONS VEGETABLE OIL

2 MEDIUM ONIONS, CHOPPED

4 GARLIC CLOVES, MINCED

2 CELERY RIBS, COARSELY CHOPPED

1 LARGE GREEN BELL PEPPER, CHOPPED

1½ CUPS CHICKEN BROTH

1 CUP CANNED CRUSHED TOMATOES

1 TEASPOON THYME

1 CUP RICE

½ CUP SLICED ALMONDS

1. In a plastic or paper bag, combine the flour, paprika, salt, black pepper, and cayenne, and shake to mix. Add the chicken and shake to coat lightly. Remove the chicken and re-serve 1 tablespoon of the seasoned flour.

2. In a large skillet, warm 1 tablespoon of the oil over medium-high heat. Add the chicken and cook until golden all over, about 4 min-utes per side. Transfer the chicken to a plate and cover loosely with foil to keep warm.

3. Add half of the onions and half of the gar-lic to the skillet and stir-fry for 1 minute. Add the celery, bell pepper, and reserved 1 table-spoon flour mixture and cook, stirring con-stantly, until the flour is no longer visible. Stir in ½ cup of the broth, the tomatoes, and thyme. Bring the mixture to a boil.

4. Return the chicken (and any juices that have collected on the plate) to the skillet and bring to a boil. Reduce the heat to medium-low, cover, and simmer until the chicken is cooked through, about 15 minutes.

5. Meanwhile, in a medium saucepan, warm the remaining 1 tablespoon oil over medium-high heat. Add the remaining onion and gar-lic; cook, stirring frequently, for 5 minutes.

6. Add the rice to the saucepan and cook, stirring, for 1 minute. Add the remaining 1 cup broth and 1 cup of water. Bring to a boil. Reduce the heat to medium-low, cover, and simmer until the rice is tender, about 20 min-utes. Stir in the almonds. Spoon the pilaf onto 4 plates and top with the chicken and sauce.

Chicken with Garlic-Vinegar Sauce

SERVES 4

1 TABLESPOON VEGETABLE OIL

3 TABLESPOONS UNSALTED BUTTER

4 LARGE UNPEELED GARLIC CLOVES

2½- TO 3-POUND CHICKEN, CUT INTO
   12 SERVING PIECES

¼ TEASPOON SALT

½ TEASPOON BLACK PEPPER

¼ CUP PLUS 1 TABLESPOON BALSAMIC
   VINEGAR OR RED WINE VINEGAR

2 MEDIUM TOMATOES, COARSELY
   CHOPPED, OR ONE 14½-OUNCE CAN
   NO-SALT-ADDED WHOLE TOMATOES,
   DRAINED AND CHOPPED

½ CUP CHICKEN BROTH

3 TABLESPOONS CHOPPED PARSLEY

1. In a large deep skillet or flameproof casserole that will hold the chicken in a single layer, warm the oil with 2 tablespoons of the butter and the garlic over medium-high heat. When the butter stops foaming, add the chicken and cook until browned on both sides, about 5 minutes.

2. Season the chicken with the salt and pepper. Add ¼ cup of the vinegar to the skillet and bring to a boil. Add the tomatoes, broth, and 2 tablespoons of the parsley, stirring to scrape up any browned bits in the bottom of the pan.

3. Return the mixture to a boil. Reduce the heat to low, cover, and simmer until the chicken is cooked through, turning once, about 15 minutes. Transfer the chicken to a serving platter and cover loosely with foil to keep warm.

4. Remove the garlic to a cutting board and push the softened cloves out of their skins. Mince the garlic and return it to the skillet, mashing slightly with the back of a spoon. Add the remaining 1 tablespoon vinegar, increase the heat to medium, and simmer, stirring constantly, until the liquid is reduced by one-third.

5. Swirl in the remaining 1 tablespoon butter until the sauce is smooth and heated through. Pour the sauce over the chicken and garnish with the remaining 1 tablespoon parsley.

CARIBBEAN CHICKEN

SERVES 4

◇ LOW - FAT

2 TABLESPOONS CORNSTARCH

½ TEASPOON BLACK PEPPER

4 SKINLESS, BONELESS CHICKEN BREAST
HALVES (ABOUT 1¼ POUNDS TOTAL)

2 TABLESPOONS VEGETABLE OIL

1 MEDIUM ONION, COARSELY CHOPPED

3 GARLIC CLOVES, MINCED

ONE 8-OUNCE CAN JUICE-PACKED
CRUSHED PINEAPPLE

¼ TEASPOON SUGAR

3 TO 5 DROPS HOT PEPPER SAUCE, TO
TASTE

1 MEDIUM GREEN BELL PEPPER,
COARSELY CHOPPED

1 MEDIUM RED OR YELLOW BELL
PEPPER, SLIVERED

2 TABLESPOONS FRESH LIME JUICE

4 TEASPOONS GRATED ORANGE ZEST

1½ TEASPOONS GRATED LIME ZEST

½ TEASPOON SALT

3 TABLESPOONS CHOPPED CILANTRO

1. In a shallow bowl, combine the cornstarch and black pepper. Lightly dredge the chicken breasts in the seasoned cornstarch.

2. In a large skillet, warm 1 tablespoon of the oil over medium-high heat. Add the chicken and brown all over, about 5 minutes per side. Transfer the chicken to a plate and cover loosely with foil to keep warm.

3. Add the remaining 1 tablespoon oil to the skillet. Add the onion, garlic, pineapple, sugar, and hot pepper sauce. Bring the mixture to a boil, reduce the heat to low, cover, and simmer for 10 minutes.

4. Return the pineapple mixture to a boil over medium-high heat. Stir in the bell peppers, lime juice, orange zest, lime zest, and salt. Return the chicken (and any juices that have collected on the plate) to the skillet. Heat until the chicken is just cooked through, about 3 minutes.

5. Stir in the cilantro. Divide the chicken and sauce among 4 plates and and serve hot.

DILLED CHICKEN WITH CHUNKY TOMATO SAUCE

SERVES 4

3 TABLESPOONS FLOUR

½ TEASPOON SALT

½ TEASPOON BLACK PEPPER

4 SKINLESS, BONELESS CHICKEN BREAST
HALVES (ABOUT 1¼ POUNDS TOTAL)

1 TABLESPOON VEGETABLE OIL

1 TABLESPOON UNSALTED BUTTER

2 SCALLIONS, COARSELY CHOPPED

1 GARLIC CLOVE, MINCED

3 LARGE PLUM TOMATOES, COARSELY
CHOPPED

⅓ CUP CHICKEN BROTH

¼ CUP DRY WHITE WINE

3 TABLESPOONS MINCED FRESH DILL,
OR 2 TEASPOONS DRIED

3 TABLESPOONS HALF-AND-HALF

1. In a plastic or paper bag, combine the flour, salt, and pepper. Add the chicken and shake to coat lightly. Remove the chicken and reserve the excess seasoned flour.

2. In a large skillet, warm the oil over medium-high heat. Add the chicken breasts and cook until golden brown on one side, about 6 minutes.

3. Turn the chicken over and cook until lightly browned on the second side, about 3 minutes longer. Transfer the chicken to a plate and cover loosely with foil to keep warm.

4. Add the butter to the skillet and heat until it melts. Add the scallions and garlic, and cook, stirring frequently, until the garlic begins to brown, about 3 minutes.

5. Stir in the reserved seasoned flour and cook, stirring constantly, until the flour is no longer visible, about 30 seconds. Add the tomatoes, broth, wine, and dill, and bring to a boil. Return the chicken (and any juices that have collected on the plate) to the skillet. Reduce the heat to medium-low, cover, and simmer for 5 minutes.

6. Turn the chicken over, stir the sauce, cover, and simmer until the chicken is cooked through, about 5 minutes.

7. Divide the chicken among 4 plates. Bring the sauce in the skillet to a boil over high heat and stir in the half-and-half until combined. Spoon the sauce on top of the chicken.

Honey-Orange Chicken

SERVES 4

◆ EXTRA-QUICK ◇ LOW-FAT

2 TABLESPOONS CORNSTARCH

½ TEASPOON SALT

⅛ TEASPOON BLACK PEPPER

4 SKINLESS, BONELESS CHICKEN BREAST
 HALVES (ABOUT 1¼ POUNDS TOTAL)

2 TABLESPOONS UNSALTED BUTTER

½ CUP CHICKEN BROTH

2 TABLESPOONS THAWED FROZEN
 ORANGE JUICE CONCENTRATE

1 TEASPOON DIJON MUSTARD

½ TEASPOON HONEY

ORANGE SLICES, FOR GARNISH

1. In a plastic or paper bag, combine the cornstarch, salt, and pepper. Add the chicken and shake to coat lightly. Remove the chicken and reserve the excess cornstarch mixture.

2. In a large skillet, melt 1 tablespoon of the butter over medium heat. Add the chicken and cook until browned on one side, about 5 minutes. Add the remaining 1 tablespoon butter, turn the chicken, and cook until browned on the second side, about 5 minutes. Transfer the chicken to a plate and cover loosely with foil to keep warm.

3. In a small bowl, combine the reserved cornstarch mixture and the broth, and whisk to blend. Whisk the broth mixture, orange juice concentrate, mustard, and honey into the skillet. Bring the mixture to a boil over medium heat, whisking constantly.

4. Return the chicken (and any juices that have collected on the plate) to the skillet. Reduce the heat to medium-low, cover, and cook until the chicken is just cooked through, 5 to 8 minutes.

5. Divide the chicken among 4 plates and serve, garnished with the orange slices.

Variation: *For a simple variation on the glaze for these sautéed chicken breasts, use frozen tangerine or apple juice concentrate instead of orange juice and maple syrup in place of the honey.*

Cider-Sautéed Chicken Breasts

SERVES 4

◆ EXTRA-QUICK

3 TABLESPOONS FLOUR

½ TEASPOON SALT

¼ TEASPOON BLACK PEPPER

¼ TEASPOON CINNAMON

4 SKINLESS, BONELESS CHICKEN BREAST
    HALVES (ABOUT 1¼ POUNDS TOTAL)

2 TABLESPOONS OLIVE OIL

1 TABLESPOON UNSALTED BUTTER

¾ TO 1¼ CUPS APPLE CIDER OR APPLE
    JUICE

1 SMALL TART UNPEELED GREEN APPLE,
    DICED

½ CUP GOLDEN RAISINS

2 TABLESPOONS HALF-AND-HALF

1. In a shallow bowl, combine the flour, salt, pepper, and cinnamon. Dredge the chicken in the seasoned flour, shaking off the excess. Reserve the excess seasoned flour.

2. In a large skillet, warm the oil with the butter over medium-high heat until the butter is melted. Add the chicken and cook until golden all over, about 3 minutes per side. Transfer the chicken to a plate and cover loosely with foil to keep warm.

3. Add the reserved seasoned flour to the skillet and cook, stirring constantly, until light golden, 2 to 3 minutes. Add ¼ cup of the cider and stir until the mixture is smooth. Stir in another ½ cup of cider, remove from the heat, and check the consistency of the sauce.

If you would prefer a thinner sauce, add up to ½ cup more cider.

4. Bring the sauce to a boil over medium-high heat. Return the chicken (and any juices that have collected on the plate) to the skillet. Add the diced apple and the raisins. Cover, reduce the heat to medium-low, and simmer for 5 minutes. Turn the chicken over and simmer, covered, until the chicken is just cooked through, about 5 minutes longer.

5. Divide the chicken among 4 plates. Stir the half-and-half into the sauce in the skillet. Spoon some of the sauce, diced apple, and raisins on top of each chicken breast.

Carbonara-Style Chicken Breasts

SERVES 4

3 SLICES BACON

2 TABLESPOONS FLOUR

½ TEASPOON SALT

½ TEASPOON BLACK PEPPER

4 SKINLESS, BONELESS CHICKEN BREAST
   HALVES (ABOUT 1¼ POUNDS TOTAL)

1 TABLESPOON UNSALTED BUTTER

4 SCALLIONS, COARSELY CHOPPED

2 GARLIC CLOVES, MINCED

1 CUP HALF-AND-HALF

¼ CUP GRATED PARMESAN CHEESE

2 TABLESPOONS CHOPPED PARSLEY
   (OPTIONAL)

1. In a large skillet, cook the bacon over medium heat until crisp, about 10 minutes. Reserving the fat in the pan, drain the bacon on paper towels; crumble and set aside.

2. Meanwhile, in a shallow bowl, combine the flour, salt, and ¼ teaspoon of the pepper. Lightly dredge the chicken breasts in the seasoned flour, shaking off the excess.

3. Warm the bacon fat over medium-high heat, add the chicken breasts, and cook until golden all over, about 4 minutes per side. Transfer the chicken to a plate and cover loosely with foil to keep warm.

4. Add the butter to the skillet and melt over medium heat. Add the scallions and garlic, and cook, stirring constantly, for 1 minute. Stir in the half-and-half, bring to a boil, and cook until slightly thickened, 1 to 2 minutes.

5. Return the chicken (and any juices that have collected on the plate) to the skillet. Reduce the heat to medium-low, partially cover, and simmer until the chicken is just cooked through, about 5 minutes.

6. Divide the chicken among 4 plates. Stir the Parmesan, parsley (if using), and remaining ¼ teaspoon pepper into the sauce in the skillet. Top each chicken breast with some of the sauce and the reserved crumbled bacon.

Chicken Breasts with Apricots and Almonds

SERVES 4

◇ LOW-FAT

3 TABLESPOONS FLOUR

2 TEASPOONS CURRY POWDER

½ TEASPOON SALT

¼ TEASPOON BLACK PEPPER

4 SKINLESS, BONELESS CHICKEN BREAST HALVES (ABOUT 1¼ POUNDS TOTAL)

1 TABLESPOON OLIVE OIL

1 TABLESPOON BUTTER

1 CUP CHICKEN BROTH, PREFERABLY REDUCED-SODIUM

½ CUP GOLDEN OR DARK RAISINS

2 TABLESPOONS TOMATO PASTE

½ TEASPOON SUGAR

½ CUP COARSELY CHOPPED DRIED APRICOTS

2 SCALLIONS, COARSELY CHOPPED

¼ CUP SLICED ALMONDS, TOASTED

1. In a plastic or paper bag, combine the flour, 1 teaspoon of the curry powder, the salt, and pepper. Add the chicken and shake to coat lightly. Remove the chicken and reserve 1 tablespoon of the excess seasoned flour.

2. In a large skillet, warm the oil with the butter over medium-high heat until the butter is melted. Add the chicken and cook until browned all over, about 5 minutes per side. Transfer the chicken to a plate and cover with foil to keep warm.

3. Stir in the reserved 1 tablespoon seasoned flour and cook over medium heat, stirring constantly, until the flour is no longer visible, about 1 minute. Stir in the broth, raisins, tomato paste, remaining 1 teaspoon curry powder, and the sugar. Bring the mixture to a boil over medium-high heat.

4. Stir in the apricots. Return the chicken (and any juices that have collected on the plate) to the skillet. Reduce the heat to medium-low, cover, and simmer, turning the chicken once, until it is just cooked through, about 5 minutes.

5. Just before serving, stir the scallions into the skillet. Serve the chicken topped with the sauce and sprinkled with the toasted almonds.

Marinated Garlic-
Oregano Chicken Breasts

SERVES 4

◇ LOW-FAT

5 GARLIC CLOVES, MINCED

¼ CUP FRESH LEMON JUICE

1½ TEASPOONS OREGANO

¼ TEASPOON BLACK PEPPER

4 SKINLESS, BONELESS CHICKEN BREAST
HALVES (ABOUT 1¼ POUNDS TOTAL)

¼ CUP CORNSTARCH

1 TABLESPOON OLIVE OIL

1 TABLESPOON UNSALTED BUTTER

1 MEDIUM ONION, CUT INTO THIN
WEDGES

¾ CUP CHICKEN BROTH, PREFERABLY
REDUCED-SODIUM

¼ CUP MINCED SCALLION GREENS

2½ TEASPOONS GRATED LEMON ZEST

PINCH OF SUGAR

1. In a shallow 11-by-7-inch baking dish, combine the garlic, lemon juice, ¾ teaspoon of the oregano, and the pepper. Add the chicken, turn to coat, and set aside to marinate for 10 minutes.

2. Meanwhile, place the cornstarch on a plate or in a shallow bowl.

3. Remove the chicken from the marinade, reserving the marinade. Dredge the chicken in the cornstarch and reserve the excess.

4. In a large skillet, warm the oil with the butter over medium-high heat until the butter is melted. Add the chicken and cook until browned all over, about 5 minutes per side. Transfer the chicken to a plate and cover loosely with foil to keep warm.

5. Add the onion to the skillet and cook, stirring frequently, until it begins to soften, about 2 minutes.

6. In a small bowl, combine the broth with the reserved cornstarch, and stir to blend. Add the broth mixture, reserved marinade, remaining ¾ teaspoon oregano, 2 tablespoons of the scallion greens, the lemon zest, and the sugar to the skillet, and bring to a boil.

7. Reduce the heat to medium. Return the chicken (and any juices that have collected on the plate) to the skillet. Cook for 2 to 3 minutes, or until the chicken is cooked through.

8. Serve the chicken topped with the onion and sauce and sprinkled with the remaining 2 tablespoons scallion greens.

Skillet Chicken Teriyaki with Fruit

SERVES 4

8 BONE-IN CHICKEN THIGHS (ABOUT
    2½ POUNDS TOTAL)
ONE 8-OUNCE CAN JUICE-PACKED
    PINEAPPLE CHUNKS
ONE 11-OUNCE CAN MANDARIN
    ORANGES
2 TABLESPOONS REDUCED-SODIUM SOY
    SAUCE

1 TABLESPOON CORNSTARCH
½ TEASPOON DRY MUSTARD
½ TEASPOON GROUND GINGER
¼ TEASPOON BLACK PEPPER
3 GARLIC CLOVES, MINCED
4 SCALLIONS, COARSELY CHOPPED

1. In a large nonstick skillet, place the chicken thighs skin-side down. Set the cold skillet on a burner. On a gas stove, start over low and gradually increase the heat to medium-high so the chicken fat is rendered. On an electric stove, set the skillet on a cold burner and turn to medium-high; in the time it takes for the element to heat up, the fat will be rendered.

2. Brown the chicken on one side, about 10 minutes. Turn the chicken over and brown on the second side, about 8 minutes.

3. Meanwhile, drain the pineapple, reserving the juice in a 1-cup measure. Drain oranges, adding enough of the syrup to the reserved pineapple juice to measure ½ cup.

4. In a small bowl, combine the fruit juice mixture, soy sauce, cornstarch, dry mustard, ginger, and pepper.

5. Transfer the chicken to a plate and cover loosely with foil to keep warm. Pour off all but 1 tablespoon fat from the skillet. Add the garlic and stir-fry over medium-high heat for 1 minute. Add the scallions and stir-fry until they are limp, 1 to 2 minutes.

6. Stir the fruit juice mixture and add it to the skillet. Add any juices that have collected on the plate under the chicken. Bring to a boil, stirring constantly, and cook until slightly thickened, 1 to 2 minutes.

7. Add the chicken and pineapple and return the mixture to a boil. Reduce the heat to low, cover, and simmer until the chicken is cooked through, about 8 minutes.

8. Stir in the mandarin oranges. Serve the chicken topped with some sauce and fruit.

CHICKEN ON A
BED OF SAUTÉED SPINACH

SERVES 4

¼ CUP FLOUR

¼ TEASPOON BLACK PEPPER

4 SKINLESS, BONELESS CHICKEN BREAST
   HALVES (ABOUT 1¼ POUNDS TOTAL)

2 TABLESPOONS OLIVE OIL

1 MEDIUM RED ONION, THINLY SLICED

1 GARLIC CLOVE, MINCED

1 POUND FRESH SPINACH, STEMMED

3 TABLESPOONS UNSALTED BUTTER

¼ TEASPOON NUTMEG

⅔ CUP CHICKEN BROTH, PREFERABLY
   REDUCED-SODIUM

⅓ CUP MILK

1 CUP SHREDDED SWISS CHEESE

1. In a shallow bowl, combine the flour and pepper. Dredge the chicken lightly in the seasoned flour, shaking off the excess; reserve the excess seasoned flour.

2. In a large broilerproof skillet, warm 1 tablespoon of the oil over medium-high heat. Add the onion and garlic, and cook, stirring, until the onion begins to brown, about 3 minutes. Add the spinach and cook, stirring, just until wilted, 2 to 3 minutes. Transfer the mixture to a plate. Cover to keep warm.

3. Add the remaining 1 tablespoon oil to the skillet and warm over medium-high heat. Add the chicken and cook until golden all over, about 4 minutes per side. Transfer the chicken to a plate and cover loosely to keep warm.

4. Add the butter to the skillet and melt over medium heat. Stir in the reserved seasoned flour and the nutmeg and cook, stirring, until the flour absorbs the butter. Gradually add the broth and milk, stirring constantly. Bring the mixture to a simmer and cook, stirring, until the sauce is slightly thickened, 1 to 2 minutes.

5. Return the chicken to the skillet and spoon the sauce on top. Bring the mixture to a boil, reduce the heat to medium-low, cover, and cook until the chicken is cooked through, 8 to 10 minutes. Meanwhile, preheat the broiler.

6. Stir ½ cup of the Swiss cheese into the sauce in the skillet. Sprinkle the remaining ½ cup Swiss cheese on top. Place the skillet under the broiler until the cheese is just golden, about 2 minutes.

7. Serve the chicken with some of the sauce on a bed of sautéed spinach and onion.

Chicken Breasts with Cilantro Sauce

SERVES 4

◆ EXTRA-QUICK

1 TABLESPOON OLIVE OIL

4 SMALL SKINLESS, BONELESS CHICKEN
   BREAST HALVES (ABOUT 1 POUND
   TOTAL)

¼ TEASPOON BLACK PEPPER

¼ TEASPOON SALT

1 TEASPOON CORNSTARCH

⅓ CUP PLAIN LOW-FAT YOGURT

2 TABLESPOONS HALF-AND-HALF

¾ CUP CHICKEN BROTH, PREFERABLY
   REDUCED-SODIUM

2 TABLESPOONS FRESH LEMON JUICE

2 GARLIC CLOVES, MINCED

2 TABLESPOONS MINCED SHALLOT OR
   SCALLION WHITES

1 SMALL TOMATO, SEEDED AND
   CHOPPED

⅓ CUP CHOPPED CILANTRO

1. In a large skillet, warm the oil over medium-high heat. Add the chicken and cook on one side until lightly browned, about 5 minutes.

2. Turn the chicken over, sprinkle with the pepper and ⅛ teaspoon of the salt, and cook until lightly browned and just cooked through, about 4 minutes. Transfer the chicken to a heated serving platter and cover loosely with foil to keep warm.

3. Meanwhile, in a small bowl, combine the cornstarch and 1 tablespoon of water and stir to blend. Stir in the yogurt and half-and-half until combined.

4. Stir the broth, lemon juice, garlic, and shallot into the skillet. Reduce the heat to low and simmer for 30 seconds. Stir in the tomato, the yogurt mixture, and the remaining ⅛ teaspoon salt, and cook for 1 minute. Remove from the heat and stir in the cilantro.

5. Spoon the sauce over the chicken and serve hot.

38

Chicken Stuffed with Broccoli, Bacon, and Cheese

SERVES 4

4 SLICES BACON

1 CUP CHOPPED COOKED FRESH OR FROZEN BROCCOLI

½ CUP SHREDDED SHARP CHEDDAR CHEESE

¼ CUP PART-SKIM RICOTTA OR SMALL-CURD COTTAGE CHEESE

2 TABLESPOONS CHOPPED PIMIENTO OR ROASTED RED PEPPER (OPTIONAL)

¼ TEASPOON BLACK PEPPER

2 WHOLE BONELESS CHICKEN BREASTS, WITH FULL SKIN ON (ABOUT 1½ POUNDS TOTAL)

ABOUT 1 TABLESPOON OLIVE OIL

1. In a medium skillet, cook the bacon over medium heat until crisp, about 10 minutes. Reserving the fat in the pan, drain the bacon on paper towels; crumble and set aside.

2. In a large bowl, combine the broccoli, Cheddar, ricotta, pimiento (if using), black pepper, and the reserved bacon. Mix well.

3. Using your fingers, make a pocket for stuffing by gently separating the chicken skin from the flesh, but keeping the skin attached at the edges.

4. With the chicken breasts skin-side down on the work surface, stuff the pockets with the broccoli-Cheddar filling (by doing this skin-side down, the weight of the chicken breast keeps the stuffing in place as you work). Pull the chicken skin up and over the filling to cover it completely. Use toothpicks to hold the skin in place on the flesh side of the breasts.

5. Pour off all but 1 tablespoon of bacon fat from the skillet. Add 1 tablespoon of the oil and warm over medium-high heat. Add the chicken breasts, skin-side up, and sear over medium-high heat for 2 minutes. Turn the breasts over and sear the other side, adding more oil if necessary to prevent sticking.

6. Reduce the heat to medium and cook the breasts, skin-side up, for 10 minutes. Turn over and cook for 5 minutes longer.

7. To serve, remove the toothpicks and cut each chicken breast in half crosswise.

HONEY-LIME CHICKEN CUTLETS

SERVES 4

♦ EXTRA-QUICK

2 TABLESPOONS OLIVE OIL

2 TABLESPOONS UNSALTED BUTTER

4 SMALL SKINLESS, BONELESS CHICKEN
BREAST HALVES (ABOUT 1 POUND
TOTAL), POUNDED ¾ INCH THICK

3 TABLESPOONS FLOUR

¾ CUP CHICKEN BROTH, PREFERABLY
REDUCED-SODIUM

⅔ CUP HONEY

1½ TEASPOONS GRATED LIME ZEST

¼ TEASPOON SALT

PINCH OF CAYENNE PEPPER

¼ CUP FRESH LIME JUICE

1. In a large skillet, warm the oil with the butter over medium-high heat until the butter is melted. Working quickly, dredge each chicken breast in flour, gently shake off the excess, and add to the skillet. Cook until browned all over, about 3 minutes per side.

2. Add the broth and bring to a boil. Reduce the heat to low, cover, and simmer until the chicken is cooked through, 3 to 5 minutes. Transfer the chicken to a warmed serving platter and cover loosely with foil to keep warm.

3. Stir the honey, lime zest, salt, and cayenne into the skillet. Increase the heat to high, bring the mixture to a rapid boil, and cook until it is reduced and slightly thickened, about 5 minutes. Remove the pan from the heat and stir in the lime juice.

4. Spoon the honey-lime sauce on top of the chicken and serve hot.

KITCHEN NOTE: *Because chicken breasts are naturally thicker on one side than the other, they are often pounded to an even thickness to speed up the cooking time and allow the chicken to cook more evenly. This step is not necessary, but it is not difficult either. No special piece of equipment is needed—just use a rolling pin or a small frying pan—and it only takes a minute or two.*

CRISPY CHICKEN AND RED BELL PEPPERS WITH LEMON

SERVES 4

◇ LOW-FAT

1 EGG

3 TABLESPOONS FLOUR

2 TABLESPOONS CORNSTARCH

1½ TEASPOONS BASIL

½ TEASPOON SALT

¼ TEASPOON BLACK PEPPER

4 SKINLESS, BONELESS CHICKEN BREAST
   HALVES (ABOUT 1¼ POUNDS
   TOTAL), POUNDED ½ INCH THICK

¼ CUP VEGETABLE OIL

1 CUP CHICKEN BROTH, PREFERABLY
   REDUCED-SODIUM

2 LARGE RED BELL PEPPERS, CUT INTO
   STRIPS

¼ CUP FRESH LEMON JUICE

2 TEASPOONS GRATED LEMON ZEST

1. In a shallow bowl, lightly beat the egg. Stir in the flour, 1 tablespoon of the cornstarch, ½ teaspoon of the basil, the salt, and black pepper, and beat until a smooth batter is formed. Lightly coat the chicken in the batter.

2. In a large skillet, warm the oil over medium-high heat. Add the chicken and cook until dark golden all over and cooked through, 4 to 5 minutes per side. Drain on paper towels. Pour all but a thin film of oil out of the skillet.

3. In a small bowl, combine the remaining 1 tablespoon cornstarch, the remaining 1 teaspoon basil, and the broth. Stir to blend.

4. Add the broth mixture, bell pepper slices, lemon juice, and lemon zest to the skillet. Bring to a boil over medium heat, stirring constantly, and cook until just thickened, about 2 minutes.

5. Slice the chicken and serve topped with the bell peppers and pan juices.

41

CHICKEN CUTLETS WITH SOUR CREAM AND JALAPEÑOS

SERVES 4

◆ EXTRA-QUICK

½ CUP REDUCED-FAT SOUR CREAM
¼ CUP SHREDDED MONTEREY JACK
   CHEESE
2 TABLESPOONS CHOPPED CILANTRO
1 TO 2 JALAPEÑO PEPPERS, MINCED
4 LARGE SKINLESS, BONELESS CHICKEN
   BREAST HALVES (ABOUT 1½ POUNDS
   TOTAL), POUNDED ½ INCH THICK

¼ TEASPOON SALT
¼ TEASPOON BLACK PEPPER
1 TABLESPOON VEGETABLE OIL
1 TABLESPOON UNSALTED BUTTER

1. In a small bowl, combine the sour cream, cheese, cilantro, and jalapeño. Stir to blend and set aside.

2. Preheat the broiler. Line a broiler rack with foil.

3. Sprinkle both sides of the chicken with the salt and black pepper.

4. In a large skillet, warm the oil with the butter over medium-high heat until the butter is melted. Add the chicken and cook until lightly browned, about 5 minutes per side. Transfer the chicken to the prepared broiler rack.

5. Top each chicken breast with a generous spoonful of the sour cream mixture. Broil 4 to 5 inches from the heat for 5 minutes, or until the chicken is cooked through and the topping bubbles. Serve hot.

CHICKEN PICCATA

SERVES 4

4 SKINLESS, BONELESS CHICKEN BREAST
   HALVES (ABOUT 1¼ POUNDS TOTAL)
1 TABLESPOON OLIVE OIL
3 TABLESPOONS UNSALTED BUTTER
½ CUP CHICKEN BROTH

3 TABLESPOONS FRESH LEMON JUICE
¼ TEASPOON SALT
¼ TEASPOON BLACK PEPPER
LEMON SLICES, FOR GARNISH

1. Remove the small "mignon" from the underside of each chicken breast half (the mignon is about 1 inch wide at its widest point and about 4 inches long) and set aside. With a large knife, cut each chicken breast in half horizontally to give you 8 cutlets and 4 mignons.

2. In a skillet large enough to hold all the chicken in a single layer (or you can cook it in 2 batches), warm the oil with 1 tablespoon of the butter over medium heat until the butter is melted. Add the chicken and cook until golden and just cooked through, 1 to 2 minutes per side. Transfer the chicken to a warmed serving platter.

3. Add the broth to the skillet. Increase the heat to high, scraping up any browned bits in the bottom of the pan, and cook until the liquid is reduced by a little more than half.

4. Add the lemon juice, salt, and pepper, and cook for 1 minute. Remove from the heat and swirl in the remaining 2 tablespoons butter until it is incorporated and the sauce is velvety.

5. Spoon the sauce over the chicken, coating it well. Garnish with lemon slices.

SUBSTITUTION: *In Step 1 above, the chicken breasts are sliced horizontally to create very thin cutlets. However, most supermarkets carry what they call "thin-sliced" chicken breast. If you can find these, it will certainly save on preparation time.*

43

Chicken Cutlets Milanese

SERVES 4

◆ EXTRA-QUICK

2 EGGS

½ CUP GRATED PARMESAN CHEESE

¼ TEASPOON SALT

¼ TEASPOON BLACK PEPPER

4 SKINLESS, BONELESS CHICKEN BREAST
HALVES (ABOUT 1¼ POUNDS
TOTAL), POUNDED ¾ INCH THICK

½ CUP FINE UNSEASONED DRY BREAD
CRUMBS

2 TABLESPOONS OLIVE OIL

2 TABLESPOONS UNSALTED BUTTER

1 SPRIG FRESH ROSEMARY, CHOPPED,
OR ½ TEASPOON DRIED

1 LEMON, CUT INTO 4 WEDGES

1. In a medium bowl, beat together the eggs, ¼ cup of the Parmesan, the salt, and pepper. Add the chicken, turn to coat, and set aside to soak for 10 minutes.

2. In a pie pan, combine the remaining ¼ cup Parmesan and the bread crumbs. Dredge each chicken breast half in the Parmesan-crumb mixture until evenly coated.

3. In a large skillet, warm the oil with the butter and rosemary over medium-high heat until the butter is melted. When the butter stops foaming, add the chicken and cook until golden brown and just cooked through, about 4 minutes per side.

4. Serve the chicken with the lemon wedges.

SWEET AFTERTHOUGHT: *This baked fruit dessert can be served warm or cold. Blend ¾ cup flour, 3 tablespoons sugar, and a pinch of salt. Beat in 4 eggs, 1⅔ cups milk, and a dash of vanilla. Pour the batter into a buttered 10-inch pie pan. Sprinkle 1 to 1½ cups green grapes over the batter and bake in a preheated 350° oven for about 35 minutes, or until golden on top and set in the center.*

Ginger-Glazed Turkey Scallopini with Sesame Rice

SERVES 4

◇ LOW-FAT

3 TABLESPOONS FLOUR

¼ TEASPOON BLACK PEPPER

4 THIN TURKEY CUTLETS (ABOUT ¾ POUND TOTAL)

1 TABLESPOON OLIVE OIL

2 CUPS CHICKEN BROTH, PREFERABLY REDUCED-SODIUM

1 CUP RICE

1 TABLESPOON REDUCED-SODIUM SOY SAUCE

5 QUARTER-SIZE SLICES FRESH GINGER, MINCED

⅓ CUP MINCED CILANTRO

2 CLOVES GARLIC, MINCED

1 TABLESPOON HONEY

1 TABLESPOON SESAME SEEDS, TOASTED

1. In a shallow bowl, combine the flour and the pepper. Lightly dredge the turkey in the seasoned flour, shaking off the excess. Reserve the excess seasoned flour.

2. In a large nonstick skillet, warm the oil over medium-high heat. Add the turkey and cook until golden brown all over, about 3 minutes per side. Transfer the turkey to a plate and cover loosely with foil to keep warm.

3. In a medium saucepan, bring 1 cup of the broth and 1 cup of water to a boil. Add the rice, reduce the heat to medium-low, cover, and simmer until the rice is tender and all the liquid is absorbed, about 20 minutes.

4. Meanwhile, in a small bowl, blend the remaining 1 cup broth with the reserved seasoned flour. Add the broth mixture to the skillet. Stir in the soy sauce and bring to a boil. Add the ginger, 3 tablespoons of the cilantro, the garlic, and honey. Reduce the heat to low, cover, and simmer the sauce for 10 minutes.

5. Return the turkey (and any juices that have collected on the plate) to the skillet. Spoon the sauce on top, cover, and simmer until heated through, about 5 minutes.

6. When the rice is done, stir in the toasted sesame seeds and the remaining cilantro. Serve the turkey with the rice and the sauce.

Chicken Cutlets with Summer Tomato Sauce

SERVES 4

1 TABLESPOON MINCED FRESH
TARRAGON

1 TABLESPOON MINCED FRESH BASIL

1 TABLESPOON MINCED PARSLEY

2 TABLESPOONS OLIVE OIL

2 LARGE TOMATOES, SEEDED AND
COARSELY CHOPPED

1 GARLIC CLOVE, MINCED

½ CUP CHICKEN BROTH

¾ TEASPOON TARRAGON VINEGAR

4 SMALL SKINLESS, BONELESS CHICKEN
BREAST HALVES (ABOUT 1 POUND
TOTAL), POUNDED ½ INCH THICK

¼ TEASPOON SALT

¼ TEASPOON WHITE PEPPER

½ CUP FINE UNSEASONED DRY BREAD
CRUMBS

2 EGG WHITES

1. In a small bowl, toss together the tarragon, basil, and parsley. Set aside.

2. In a small saucepan, warm 1 tablespoon of the oil over medium-high heat. Add the tomatoes and garlic, and cook, stirring frequently, until softened, about 5 minutes.

3. Add the broth, vinegar, and 2 tablespoons of the herb mixture. Bring the mixture to a boil, reduce the heat to medium-low, cover, and simmer for 5 minutes. Transfer the sauce to a food processor or blender and process until puréed. Return the sauce to the pan and cover to keep warm.

4. Meanwhile, season the chicken on both sides with the salt and pepper. On a large plate, blend the remaining herb mixture with the bread crumbs. In a shallow bowl, whisk the egg whites vigorously. Dip the chicken in the whites, then in the bread crumb mixture, turning to coat.

5. In a large skillet, warm remaining tablespoon of oil over medium-high heat. Add the chicken and cook until lightly browned on one side, about 3 minutes. Turn the breasts over, cover the skillet loosely, and cook until the chicken is lightly browned and cooked through, about 4 minutes.

6. Serve the chicken topped with the tomato-herb sauce.

Turkey Scallopini with Peppers and Mushrooms

SERVES 4

◆ EXTRA-QUICK ◇ LOW-FAT

2 TABLESPOONS FLOUR

¾ TEASPOON OREGANO

½ TEASPOON SALT

¼ TEASPOON BLACK PEPPER

4 TURKEY CUTLETS (ABOUT 1 POUND TOTAL)

1 TABLESPOON OLIVE OIL

1 MEDIUM RED BELL PEPPER, CUT INTO THIN STRIPS

1 MEDIUM GREEN OR YELLOW BELL PEPPER, CUT INTO THIN STRIPS

¼ POUND MUSHROOMS, SLICED

½ CUP CHICKEN BROTH

1. In a plastic or paper bag, combine the flour, ½ teaspoon of the oregano, the salt, and black pepper. Add the turkey cutlets and lightly dredge them in the seasoned flour, shaking off the excess.

2. In a large nonstick skillet, warm the oil over medium-high heat. Add the turkey and cook until lightly golden, about 2 minutes per side. Transfer the turkey to a plate and cover loosely with foil to keep warm.

3. Add the bell peppers, mushrooms, broth, and remaining ¼ teaspoon oregano to the skillet. Reduce the heat to medium, cover, and simmer for 3 minutes.

4. Return the turkey (and any juices that have collected on the plate) to the pan. Increase the heat to medium-high, cover, and cook until the turkey is just heated through, about 2 minutes.

5. Divide the turkey and vegetables among 4 plates, spoon some of the pan juices on top, and serve hot.

TURKEY CUTLETS WITH LEMON SLICES

SERVES 4

◆ EXTRA-QUICK

2 LEMONS
2 GARLIC CLOVES, MINCED
¼ CUP CHOPPED PARSLEY (OPTIONAL)
3 TABLESPOONS FLOUR
½ TEASPOON SALT

¼ TEASPOON BLACK PEPPER
8 SMALL TURKEY CUTLETS (ABOUT
  1½ POUNDS TOTAL)
2 TABLESPOONS OLIVE OIL
4 TABLESPOONS UNSALTED BUTTER

1. Cut one lemon into very thin slices (use whichever lemon has thinner skin). Juice the remaining lemon. Set the lemon slices and juice aside.

2. In a shallow bowl, combine the garlic, parsley (if using), flour, salt, and pepper. Dredge the turkey in the seasoned flour, shaking off the excess.

3. In a large skillet, warm 1 tablespoon of the oil with 1 tablespoon of the butter over medium-high heat until the butter is melted. Add as many turkey cutlets as will fit without crowding and cook until golden brown all over and just cooked through, about 3 minutes per side. Transfer the sautéed turkey to a

platter and cover loosely with foil to keep warm while you cook the rest of the turkey in the remaining 1 tablespoon oil and 1 tablespoon of the butter.

4. When all of the turkey has been cooked, add the remaining 2 tablespoons butter and the lemon juice to the skillet. Increase the heat to high and cook, stirring constantly, for 1 minute.

5. Add the lemon slices and cook for 30 seconds. Arrange the lemon slices over the turkey and pour the lemon sauce on top.

TURKEY CUTLETS WITH TOMATO-HORSERADISH SAUCE

SERVES 4

⅓ CUP FLOUR

½ TEASPOON BLACK PEPPER

1 EGG WHITE

4 TURKEY CUTLETS (ABOUT 1 POUND TOTAL)

2 TABLESPOONS OLIVE OIL

2 TABLESPOONS UNSALTED BUTTER

3 GARLIC CLOVES, MINCED

1 MEDIUM ONION, COARSELY CHOPPED

2 CELERY RIBS, COARSELY CHOPPED

1 MEDIUM GREEN BELL PEPPER, COARSELY CHOPPED

1 CUP CANNED NO-SALT-ADDED WHOLE TOMATOES, WITH THEIR JUICE

3 TABLESPOONS HORSERADISH

¾ TEASPOON BASIL

½ TEASPOON SUGAR

½ TEASPOON SALT

PINCH OF CAYENNE PEPPER

1. In a shallow bowl, combine the flour and black pepper. In another shallow bowl, lightly beat the egg white.

2. Dip the turkey cutlets in the egg white, then lightly dredge them in the seasoned flour, shaking off the excess. Reserve 1 tablespoon of the excess seasoned flour.

3. In a large skillet, warm 1 tablespoon of the oil with 1 tablespoon of the butter over medium-high heat until the butter is melted. Add the turkey and cook until golden, about 3 minutes per side. Transfer the turkey to a plate and cover loosely to keep warm.

4. Add the remaining 1 tablespoon oil to the skillet. Add the garlic and onion, and cook, stirring frequently, until the onion begins to brown, about 5 minutes.

5. Add the remaining 1 tablespoon butter and the reserved 1 tablespoon seasoned flour. Cook, stirring constantly, until the flour is no longer visible, about 30 seconds.

6. Add the celery, bell pepper, tomatoes, horseradish, basil, sugar, salt, and cayenne, and bring to a boil, breaking up the tomatoes with the back of a spoon. Reduce the heat to medium and simmer, stirring frequently, for 5 minutes.

7. Increase the heat to medium-high and return the sauce to a boil. Add the turkey (and any juices that have collected on the plate) to the skillet and cook until the turkey is heated through, about 2 minutes.

TURKEY HASH WITH CHILIES

SERVES 4

3 TABLESPOONS FLOUR

1½ POUNDS SKINLESS, BONELESS
TURKEY BREAST, CUT INTO
¾-INCH CUBES

3 TABLESPOONS UNSALTED BUTTER

1 POUND ALL-PURPOSE POTATOES,
PEELED AND CUT INTO
¾-INCH CUBES

1 MEDIUM ONION, DICED

1 GARLIC CLOVE, MINCED

1 CUP HALF-AND-HALF

TWO 4-OUNCE CANS MILD GREEN
CHILIES, DRAINED AND CUT INTO
THIN STRIPS

¼ TEASPOON SALT

¼ TEASPOON WHITE PEPPER

2 TABLESPOONS MINCED CILANTRO
(OPTIONAL)

1. Place the flour in a medium bowl. Add the turkey and toss to coat thoroughly. Shake off any excess flour.

2. In a large skillet, melt the butter over medium-high heat. Add the turkey, potatoes, onion, and garlic, and cook, stirring constantly, until the turkey is no longer pink, 4 to 5 minutes.

3. Continue cooking until the turkey and potatoes are well browned, about 15 minutes; turn with a spatula every 5 minutes.

4. Stir in the half-and-half, reduce the heat to medium-low, and cook until the turkey and potatoes are tender and the sauce is slightly thickened, 5 to 10 minutes.

5. Stir in the chilies, salt, and pepper. Serve sprinkled with the cilantro, if desired.

SUBSTITUTION: *In place of the canned green chilies, use a coarsely chopped green bell pepper and add it in Step 2 along with the onion. To replace the spiciness of the chilies, add a pinch of cayenne to the flour used to dredge the turkey.*

STIR-FRIED
CHICKEN WITH CASHEW NUTS

SERVES 4

¾ POUND SKINLESS, BONELESS
CHICKEN BREASTS, SLICED ACROSS
THE GRAIN INTO THIN STRIPS

¾ TEASPOON WHITE PEPPER

½ TEASPOON SALT

1 TABLESPOON REDUCED-SODIUM SOY
SAUCE

1 TABLESPOON DRY SHERRY

2 TEASPOONS CORNSTARCH

¼ CUP OLIVE OIL

5 QUARTER-SIZE SLICES FRESH GINGER

5 GARLIC CLOVES, BRUISED AND PEELED

2 CUPS BROCCOLI PIECES—FLORETS
LEFT WHOLE, STEMS THINLY SLICED

2 CARROTS, THINLY SLICED

6 WATER CHESTNUTS, SLICED

3 SCALLIONS, SLICED DIAGONALLY

1 SMALL RED ONION, CHOPPED

2 TABLESPOONS UNSALTED CASHEWS

½ CUP CHICKEN BROTH

¼ TEASPOON ORIENTAL (DARK) SESAME
OIL

1. In a medium bowl, sprinkle the chicken with ½ teaspoon of the pepper and ¼ teaspoon of the salt; toss well. In a cup, blend the soy sauce, sherry, and cornstarch. Set aside.

2. Heat a large skillet over medium-high heat. Gradually pour 2 tablespoons of the olive oil into the skillet.

3. Add the ginger and garlic, and stir-fry for 30 seconds. Add the chicken and stir-fry until the meat turns white, about 3 minutes. With a slotted spoon, transfer the chicken mixture to a plate. Discard the ginger and garlic.

4. Pour 1 tablespoon of the olive oil into the skillet. Add the broccoli, carrots, and remaining ¼ teaspoon each pepper and salt. Pour in the remaining 1 tablespoon olive oil. Add the water chestnuts, scallions, onion, and cashews, and stir-fry for 2 minutes.

5. Return the chicken to the skillet and toss well. Push the contents to the sides and pour the broth into the center. Stir the cornstarch mixture to recombine, then stir it into the broth and cook, stirring constantly, until the sauce thickens. Toss the chicken and vegetables with the sauce, add the sesame oil, stir well, and serve hot.

Chicken Strips Véronique

SERVES 4

◆ EXTRA-QUICK

2 TABLESPOONS FLOUR

½ TEASPOON SALT

¼ TEASPOON BLACK PEPPER

1½ POUNDS SKINLESS, BONELESS
   CHICKEN BREASTS, SLICED ACROSS
   THE GRAIN INTO ½-INCH-WIDE
   STRIPS

2 TABLESPOONS OLIVE OIL

2 TABLESPOONS UNSALTED BUTTER

2 CUPS SEEDLESS GREEN GRAPES

½ CUP CHICKEN BROTH

½ CUP HALF-AND-HALF

2 TABLESPOONS DRY WHITE WINE
   (OPTIONAL)

1. In a shallow bowl, combine the flour, salt, and pepper. Add the chicken strips to the seasoned flour and toss to coat lightly.

2. In a large skillet, warm the oil with the butter over medium-high heat until the butter is melted. Add the chicken strips and stir-fry just until the chicken begins to brown, 3 to 4 minutes.

3. Add the grapes, broth, half-and-half, and wine (if using). Bring the mixture to a boil, reduce the heat to medium-low, cover, and simmer, stirring occasionally, until the chicken is cooked through and the grapes are slightly softened, 3 to 4 minutes.

4. Divide the chicken mixture among 4 plates and serve hot.

Substitution: *As in sole Véronique (the classic French fish dish that inspired this recipe), white wine is called for to make the sauce. If you do not already have an open bottle of wine on hand, just add a bit more chicken broth in its place.*

TURKEY STIR-FRY WITH CORN AND BROCCOLI

SERVES 4

◆ EXTRA-QUICK ◇ LOW-FAT

2 CUPS CHICKEN BROTH, PREFERABLY
   REDUCED-SODIUM

¾ CUP RICE

2 TABLESPOONS FLOUR

½ TEASPOON SALT

¼ TEASPOON BLACK PEPPER

½ POUND TURKEY CUTLETS, CUT INTO
   ¼-INCH-WIDE STRIPS

1 TABLESPOON OLIVE OIL

2 MEDIUM STALKS BROCCOLI, CUT
   INTO BITE-SIZE PIECES

1 MEDIUM RED ONION, THINLY SLICED

1 CUP FROZEN CORN, THAWED

3 GARLIC CLOVES, MINCED

3 TABLESPOONS FRESH LEMON JUICE

1 TEASPOON GRATED LEMON ZEST

¾ TEASPOON THYME

1. In a medium saucepan, bring 1¾ cups of the broth to a boil. Stir in the rice, reduce the heat to medium-low, cover, and simmer until the rice is tender, about 20 minutes.

2. Meanwhile, in a shallow bowl, combine the flour, salt, and pepper. Lightly dredge the turkey strips in the seasoned flour; shake off the excess seasoned flour.

3. In a large nonstick skillet, warm the oil over medium-high heat. Add the turkey strips and stir-fry until the meat is no longer pink, about 6 minutes. Transfer the turkey to a plate and cover loosely with foil to keep warm.

4. Add the remaining ¼ cup broth to the skillet. Add the broccoli, onion, corn, and garlic, and stir-fry for 2 minutes. Add the lemon juice, lemon zest, and thyme, and bring to a boil. Reduce the heat to medium-low, cover, and simmer until the vegetables are just tender, about 5 minutes.

5. Return the turkey (and any juices that have collected on the plate) to the skillet, add the cooked rice, and toss well to combine. Serve hot.

Chicken-Vegetable Stir-Fry with Walnuts

SERVES 4

◆ EXTRA-QUICK

10 OUNCES SKINLESS, BONELESS
CHICKEN BREASTS, CUT INTO
1-INCH CUBES

3 TABLESPOONS VEGETABLE OIL

2 TABLESPOONS REDUCED-SODIUM SOY
SAUCE

1½ TABLESPOONS CORNSTARCH

¾ CUP CHICKEN BROTH

½ TEASPOON SUGAR

¼ TEASPOON RED PEPPER FLAKES

1 LARGE RED BELL PEPPER, CUT INTO
1-INCH SQUARES

1 LARGE STALK BROCCOLI, CUT INTO
BITE-SIZE PIECES

1 MEDIUM RED ONION, THINLY SLICED

2 GARLIC CLOVES, MINCED

ONE 8-OUNCE CAN SLICED WATER
CHESTNUTS, DRAINED

¼ CUP WALNUT HALVES OR PIECES

1. Place the chicken in a bowl. Add 1 tablespoon each of the oil, soy sauce, and cornstarch. Toss to thoroughly coat the chicken and set aside.

2. In a small bowl, combine the broth, sugar, red pepper flakes, and the remaining 1 tablespoon soy sauce. Stir in the remaining 1½ teaspoons cornstarch until blended. Set aside.

3. In a large skillet or wok, warm 1 tablespoon of the oil over medium-high heat. Add the chicken and its marinade and stir-fry until the chicken is opaque but still slightly pink in the center, 2 to 3 minutes. Transfer the chicken to a plate and set aside.

4. Add the remaining 1 tablespoon oil to the skillet. Add the bell pepper, broccoli, onion, garlic, and water chestnuts, and stir-fry until the onion begins to wilt, 2 to 3 minutes.

5. Return the chicken (and any juices that have collected on the plate) to the skillet and add the walnuts. Stir the broth-cornstarch mixture and add it to the skillet. Bring the mixture to a boil and cook, stirring constantly, until the vegetables are crisp-tender and the chicken is cooked through, 2 to 3 minutes longer. Serve hot.

54

Orange Chicken with Oriental Noodles

SERVES 4

◆ EXTRA-QUICK

1 TABLESPOON CORNSTARCH

¼ TEASPOON BLACK PEPPER

1 POUND SKINLESS, BONELESS CHICKEN
BREASTS, SLICED ACROSS THE GRAIN
INTO THIN STRIPS

1 TABLESPOON ORIENTAL (DARK)
SESAME OIL

Two 3½-OUNCE PACKAGES INSTANT
RAMEN NOODLES

2 TABLESPOONS VEGETABLE OIL

3 CUPS SHREDDED CABBAGE

4 QUARTER-SIZE SLICES FRESH GINGER,
MINCED

3 GARLIC CLOVES, MINCED

ONE 8-OUNCE CAN SLICED WATER
CHESTNUTS, DRAINED

4 SCALLIONS, CUT INTO 1-INCH PIECES

ONE 11-OUNCE CAN MANDARIN
ORANGES, DRAINED

3 TABLESPOONS REDUCED-SODIUM SOY
SAUCE

1. In a plastic or paper bag, combine the cornstarch and pepper, and shake to mix. Add the chicken and shake to coat lightly. Remove the chicken to a bowl, sprinkle with the sesame oil, and toss well to coat.

2. In a large saucepan, bring 1½ quarts of water and the seasoning packets from the ramen to a boil.

3. Meanwhile, in a large skillet, warm 1 tablespoon of the vegetable oil over medium-high heat. Add the chicken and stir-fry until the meat is no longer pink, 3 to 4 minutes. Transfer the chicken to a plate and cover loosely with foil to keep warm.

4. Add the remaining 1 tablespoon vegetable oil to the skillet. Add the cabbage, ginger, garlic, and water chestnuts, and stir-fry until the cabbage is wilted, about 3 minutes.

5. Meanwhile, add the ramen noodles (breaking them up a bit) to the boiling water and cook according to package directions. Drain well.

6. Return the chicken (and any juices that have collected on the plate) to the skillet. Add the drained noodles, scallions, mandarin oranges, and soy sauce. Toss well to combine and serve at once.

HOT AND SPICY
CHICKEN WITH RED CABBAGE

SERVES 4

¼ CUP FINELY CHOPPED PITTED PRUNES

2 GARLIC CLOVES, MINCED

½ TO 1 TEASPOON RED PEPPER FLAKES,
   TO TASTE

2 TABLESPOONS OLIVE OIL

¾ POUND SKINLESS, BONELESS
   CHICKEN BREASTS, SLICED ACROSS
   THE GRAIN INTO ½-INCH-WIDE
   STRIPS

⅓ POUND FRESH THIN GREEN BEANS

1 TABLESPOON REDUCED-SODIUM SOY
   SAUCE

1 SMALL HEAD RED CABBAGE, CUT
   INTO 2-INCH-LONG STRIPS

¼ TEASPOON SALT

6 SCALLIONS, HALVED LENGTHWISE
   AND CUT INTO 2-INCH-LONG STRIPS

1. In a large, shallow dish, combine the prunes, garlic, red pepper flakes, and 1½ teaspoons of the oil. Add the chicken and set aside to marinate for 30 minutes, stirring occasionally to coat the chicken.

2. Meanwhile, in a medium saucepan of boiling water, blanch the green beans for 1 minute. Rinse the beans under cold running water, then place them in a bowl and add the soy sauce. Set aside to marinate, turning occasionally to coat the beans.

3. Place a wok or large skillet over high heat and add 1 tablespoon of the oil. Add the cabbage and salt, and stir-fry until the cabbage

wilts, about 3 minutes. Add the green beans with the soy sauce and half the scallions. Continue stir-frying for 3 minutes. Transfer the cabbage mixture to a large bowl.

4. Add the remaining 1½ teaspoons oil to the wok and warm over medium-high heat. Add the chicken and its marinade along with the remaining scallions, and stir-fry until the chicken is no longer pink, about 4 minutes. Return the cabbage mixture to the pan, mix well, and serve hot.

56

Stir-Fried Turkey with Mixed Vegetables

SERVES 4

3 TABLESPOONS PLUS 1 TEASPOON
   REDUCED-SODIUM SOY SAUCE

2 TABLESPOONS MINCED FRESH GINGER

2 TEASPOONS ORIENTAL (DARK)
   SESAME OIL

2 GARLIC CLOVES, MINCED

¾ POUND SKINLESS, BONELESS TURKEY
   BREAST, CUT INTO 2½-BY-½-INCH
   STRIPS

½ CUP CHICKEN BROTH

1 TABLESPOON RED WINE VINEGAR

1 TABLESPOON SESAME SEEDS

¼ TEASPOON BLACK PEPPER

4 TEASPOONS VEGETABLE OIL

1 SMALL RED BELL PEPPER, CUT INTO
   ¼-INCH-WIDE STRIPS

1 CUP SMALL BROCCOLI FLORETS

½ CUP THINLY SLICED MUSHROOMS

¼ CUP SNOW PEAS, FRESH OR THAWED
   FROZEN

4 SCALLIONS, COARSELY CHOPPED

1 CUP SLICED NAPA CABBAGE

1. In a medium bowl, combine 2 tablespoons of the soy sauce, the ginger, 1 teaspoon of the sesame oil, and the garlic. Add the turkey, toss to combine, and set aside to marinate for about 30 minutes.

2. In a small bowl, combine the broth, vinegar, sesame seeds, and black pepper. Stir in the remaining 1 tablespoon plus 1 teaspoon soy sauce and 1 teaspoon sesame oil until well blended. Set aside.

3. Place a wok or large skillet over high heat and add 2 teaspoons of the vegetable oil. Add the turkey and stir-fry just until the meat is

opaque, about 2 minutes. Remove the wok from the heat. Transfer the turkey to a plate and cover loosely with foil to keep warm.

4. Heat the remaining 2 teaspoons vegetable oil in the wok. Add the bell pepper, broccoli, mushrooms, and snow peas, and stir-fry for 1 minute. Add the scallions and cabbage, and stir-fry for 1 minute.

5. Pour in the broth mixture and stir-fry the mixture for 2 minutes. Return the turkey (and any juices that have collected on the plate) to the wok and heat through. Serve hot.

Fajitas with Stir-Fried Chicken

SERVES 4

◆ EXTRA-QUICK

1 POUND SKINLESS, BONELESS CHICKEN
   BREASTS, SLICED ACROSS THE GRAIN
   INTO THIN STRIPS
½ CUP FRESH LEMON JUICE
6 TABLESPOONS CHOPPED CILANTRO
   OR PARSLEY
1 TABLESPOON PLUS 1 TEASPOON
   CUMIN
2 TEASPOONS CORNSTARCH

1 TEASPOON SALT
½ TEASPOON BLACK PEPPER
8 FLOUR TORTILLAS
1 CUP MILD RED OR GREEN SALSA
2 TABLESPOONS VEGETABLE OIL
8 LARGE ROMAINE LETTUCE LEAVES,
   SHREDDED
½ CUP REDUCED-FAT SOUR CREAM

1. Preheat the oven to 200°.

2. Place the chicken in a small bowl. Add ¼ cup plus 2 tablespoons of the lemon juice, 2 tablespoons of the cilantro, the cumin, cornstarch, salt, and pepper and mix gently until the chicken is well coated; set aside.

3. Stack the tortillas and wrap them in foil. Place them in the oven to warm for 5 to 10 minutes.

4. Meanwhile, in a small bowl, stir together the salsa and the remaining 2 tablespoons lemon juice and 4 tablespoons cilantro. Set the sauce aside.

5. In a medium skillet, warm the oil over medium-high heat. Add the chicken and sauté until white and firm, about 5 minutes.

6. Place the tortillas, chicken, lettuce, sauce, and sour cream in serving dishes. Let each diner assemble the fajitas by topping a tortilla with some of each of the ingredients, ending with a dollop of sour cream, and then rolling it up.

CHICKEN WITH WHITE WINE, ROSEMARY, AND PEPPERS

SERVES 4

¼ CUP FLOUR

¼ TEASPOON SALT

¼ TEASPOON BLACK PEPPER

2½ TO 3 POUNDS CHICKEN PARTS

2 TABLESPOONS OLIVE OIL

2 TO 3 GARLIC CLOVES, PEELED

½ CUP DRY WHITE WINE OR DRY VERMOUTH

2 MEDIUM RED BELL PEPPERS, CUT INTO ¼-INCH-WIDE STRIPS

2 SPRIGS FRESH ROSEMARY, CHOPPED, OR 1½ TEASPOONS DRIED

1. Preheat the oven to 375°. Lightly oil a roasting pan.

2. In a plastic or paper bag, combine the flour, salt, and ⅛ teaspoon of the black pepper. Add the chicken parts and lightly dredge them in the seasoned flour, shaking off the excess.

3. In a large skillet, warm the oil over medium-high heat. Add the garlic and cook, stirring frequently, until golden brown, 2 to 3 minutes. Discard the garlic.

4. Add the chicken to the skillet in a single layer, skin-side down, increase the heat to high, and cook until one side is golden brown, 3 to 4 minutes. Turn the chicken over

and cook the other side until golden brown, 3 to 4 minutes. Transfer the chicken pieces to the prepared roasting pan and set aside.

5. Pour off all but a thin layer of fat from the skillet and return to medium heat. Add the wine, increase the heat to medium-high, and boil until the liquid is reduced by half, 1 to 2 minutes. Reduce the heat to medium, add the bell peppers and rosemary, and cook, stirring constantly, for 2 minutes.

6. Spoon the bell pepper mixture over the chicken, sprinkle with the remaining ⅛ teaspoon black pepper, and bake for 15 minutes, or until the chicken is just cooked through.

Chicken with Orange and Onion

SERVES 8

Two 3-pound chickens, quartered
    and skinned, wings removed
2 tablespoons·flour
½ teaspoon salt
¼ teaspoon black pepper
2 tablespoons olive oil
4 teaspoons grated orange zest

3 medium onions, thinly sliced
2 teaspoons chopped fresh thyme,
    or ½ teaspoon dried
1¾ cups orange juice
¾ cup dry white wine
2 tablespoons fresh lemon juice
1 tablespoon honey

1. Dust the chicken quarters with the flour; shake off the excess. Sprinkle them with ¼ teaspoon of the salt and ⅛ teaspoon of the pepper.

2. In a large nonstick skillet, warm the oil over medium-high heat. Add the chicken in several batches, and sauté until golden brown on all sides, about 10 minutes. Transfer the pieces to a 13-by-9-inch baking dish and scatter the orange zest over them. Reserve the oil in the skillet.

3. Preheat the oven to 350°. Warm the reserved oil in the skillet over medium-low heat. Add the onions and cook, stirring occasionally, until translucent, about 10 minutes.

Stir in the thyme and the remaining ¼ teaspoon salt and ⅛ teaspoon pepper, and remove from the heat. Spread the mixture over the chicken quarters.

4. Add the orange juice, wine, lemon juice, and honey to the skillet. Bring the liquid to a boil over high heat and cook until reduced to approximately 1 cup. Pour the liquid over the chicken.

5. Bake the chicken for about 35 minutes, basting once or twice with the pan liquid, or until the juices run clear when a thigh is pierced with the tip of a sharp knife.

Honey-Basil Chicken

SERVES 4

4 WHOLE CHICKEN LEGS (DRUMSTICK
  AND THIGH), SKINNED
¼ TEASPOON SALT
¼ TEASPOON BLACK PEPPER
1 TABLESPOON OLIVE OIL

1 TABLESPOON UNSALTED BUTTER
2 TABLESPOONS HONEY
2 TABLESPOONS CHICKEN BROTH
2 GARLIC CLOVES, THINLY SLICED
30 TO 40 FRESH BASIL LEAVES

1. Preheat the oven to 400°. Cut 4 pieces of foil 12 inches square. Sprinkle the chicken legs with the salt and pepper.

2. In a large skillet, warm the oil with the butter over medium heat. Add the chicken and brown all over, about 2 minutes per side.

3. Place a chicken leg in the middle of each foil square. Drizzle 1½ teaspoons of the honey and 1½ teaspoons of the broth over each one. Lay one-fourth of the garlic slices on each piece, cover with a layer of the basil leaves, and wrap the foil snugly over the top.

4. Place the foil packages on a baking sheet and bake for 30 minutes. Remove a foil package from the oven and unwrap it carefully to preserve the juices. Test for doneness by piercing the thigh with the tip of a sharp knife to see if the juices run clear. If the juices are still pinkish, rewrap the packages and bake about 5 minutes more.

5. To serve, unwrap each package and transfer the chicken legs to a platter. Remove any garlic or basil that sticks to the foil and put it back on the chicken. Pour the collected juices from the foil packages over the legs.

Substitution: *If you would prefer to make these with chicken breasts instead of legs, use large bone-in chicken breasts, skinned. Or, if you have only boneless breasts on hand, note that the baking times will be shorter than for bone-in chicken.*

Spiced Oven-Fried Chicken

SERVES 4

¼ CUP FLOUR

½ TEASPOON SALT

½ TEASPOON WHITE PEPPER

3 EGG WHITES

1 TEASPOON CINNAMON

¼ TEASPOON TURMERIC

1 CUP FRESH BREAD CRUMBS

ONE 3-POUND CHICKEN, QUARTERED
AND SKINNED

2 TABLESPOONS OLIVE OIL

1. Preheat the oven to 325°. On a plate, mix the flour, salt, and pepper. In a small bowl, whisk the egg whites, cinnamon, and turmeric until well blended. Spread the bread crumbs on a sheet of waxed paper.

2. Dredge the chicken quarters in the seasoned flour, shaking off the excess, then dip them in the egg whites and coat them with the bread crumbs.

3. In an ovenproof skillet large enough to hold the chicken in a single layer, heat the oil over medium heat. Lay the chicken, bone-side up, in the skillet and brown lightly on one side, about 2 minutes. Turn the chicken over, put the skillet in the oven, and bake for 30 minutes.

4. Remove the skillet and increase the oven temperature to 450°. Wait about 5 minutes, then place the skillet in the oven and allow the coating to crisp for 4 to 5 minutes, taking care not to burn it.

KITCHEN NOTE: *To make the 1 cup fresh bread crumbs called for, use your fingers to crumble 2 slices of bread into small pieces. If the bread is a little bit stale, it makes it easier to crumble.*

LAYERED TURKEY ENCHILADA CASSEROLE

SERVES 6

ONE 16-OUNCE CAN TOMATO SAUCE
ONE 4-OUNCE CAN CHOPPED MILD
    GREEN CHILIES, DRAINED
1 GARLIC CLOVE, MINCED
1 TABLESPOON CHILI POWDER
2 TEASPOONS CUMIN
1 TEASPOON OREGANO
¼ TEASPOON BLACK PEPPER

9 CORN TORTILLAS
½ POUND ROAST TURKEY, CUT INTO
    2-BY-¼-INCH STRIPS
8 SCALLIONS, COARSELY CHOPPED
ONE 10-OUNCE PACKAGE FROZEN
    CORN, THAWED
2½ CUPS SHREDDED CHEDDAR CHEESE

1. Preheat the oven to 375°. Lightly grease a shallow 1-quart baking dish.

2. In a medium bowl, combine the tomato sauce, green chilies, garlic, chili powder, cumin, oregano, and black pepper.

3. Line the bottom of the prepared baking dish with 3 tortillas, overlapping them. Spread one-third of the tomato-chili sauce over the tortillas.

4. Cover the tortillas with half the turkey, half the scallions, and half the corn. Sprinkle with 1 cup of the Cheddar.

5. Top with 3 more tortillas, overlapping them, then half the remaining tomato-chili sauce, and all the remaining turkey, scallions, and corn. Sprinkle with 1 cup of the Cheddar. Top with the remaining 3 tortillas, the remaining tomato-chili sauce, and the remaining ½ cup Cheddar.

6. Bake the casserole, uncovered, for 25 minutes, or until thoroughly heated.

Spinach-Stuffed Chicken Breasts

SERVES 4

1 TABLESPOON PLUS 1 TEASPOON OLIVE
   OIL
1 TABLESPOON UNSALTED BUTTER
1 MEDIUM ONION, FINELY CHOPPED
1 POUND SPINACH, STEMMED AND
   COARSELY CHOPPED
½ CUP PART-SKIM RICOTTA CHEESE
½ CUP GRATED PARMESAN CHEESE
1 TEASPOON MINCED FRESH BASIL
¼ TEASPOON BLACK PEPPER

1 CUP PLAIN LOW-FAT YOGURT
1 TABLESPOON RED WINE VINEGAR
½ TEASPOON SALT
1 MEDIUM TOMATO, FINELY CHOPPED
4 LARGE BASIL LEAVES, THINLY SLICED
4 BONELESS CHICKEN BREAST HALVES
   (ABOUT 1¼ POUNDS TOTAL), WITH
   SKIN INTACT
1 TEASPOON CHOPPED FRESH THYME,
   OR ¼ TEASPOON DRIED

1. In a large skillet, warm 1 tablespoon of the oil with the butter over medium heat until the butter is melted. Add the onion and cook, stirring frequently, until translucent, about 5 minutes. Add the spinach and cook until wilted, about 6 minutes. Transfer the mixture to a bowl to cool, then stir in the ricotta, Parmesan, minced basil, and ⅛ teaspoon of the pepper.

2. In a small serving bowl, blend the yogurt, vinegar, and ¼ teaspoon of the salt. Stir in the tomato, sliced basil, and remaining ⅛ teaspoon pepper. Set the sauce aside.

3. Preheat the oven to 375°. Lightly oil a baking dish just large enough to hold the chicken in a single layer.

4. Loosen the skin of each chicken breast but leave the skin attached on one side. Rub the thyme and the remaining ¼ teaspoon salt into the flesh. Drizzle ¼ teaspoon of the olive oil onto the skin of each breast.

5. Neatly fill each pocket between the skin and flesh with one-fourth of the spinach stuffing. Place the breasts, skin-side up, in the prepared baking dish and bake for 25 minutes, or until the skin is golden brown.

6. Transfer the chicken to a cutting board. Cut each breast into thin slices and arrange them on 4 plates. Serve with the yogurt sauce.

Foil-Baked Chicken with Onion and Yellow Pepper

SERVES 4

◇ LOW-FAT

4 SKINLESS, BONELESS CHICKEN BREAST
   HALVES (ABOUT 1¼ POUNDS TOTAL)
1 MEDIUM YELLOW, RED, OR GREEN
   BELL PEPPER, CUT INTO THIN STRIPS
1 SMALL RED ONION, CUT INTO THIN
   RINGS

½ TEASPOON SALT
¼ TEASPOON BLACK PEPPER
1 TABLESPOON ORIENTAL (DARK)
   SESAME OIL

1. Preheat the oven to 375°. Cut four 12-inch squares of foil.

2. Place a chicken breast half in the center of each foil square and top the chicken with the bell pepper and onion. Sprinkle with the salt and black pepper. Drizzle the chicken and vegetables with the sesame oil.

3. Fold the foil over the chicken and vegetables, then fold and crimp the edges together to seal them. Place the packets on a baking sheet and bake for 20 to 25 minutes, or until the chicken is opaque.

4. To serve, open the packets and carefully slide the chicken, vegetables, and juices onto 4 plates and serve hot.

Variation: *To give this foil-baked chicken a completely different flavor, replace the sesame oil with olive oil (as deeply flavored as you can get) and add ¼ teaspoon crumbled tarragon to each packet.*

SOUTHERN-STYLE CURRIED CHICKEN PACKETS

SERVES 4

◇ LOW-FAT

1 TABLESPOON OLIVE OIL

4 MEDIUM SHALLOTS OR 1 SMALL ONION, FINELY CHOPPED

3 GARLIC CLOVES, MINCED

1 LARGE CARROT, COARSELY CHOPPED

¼ POUND MUSHROOMS, COARSELY CHOPPED

2 TABLESPOONS CURRY POWDER

2 TABLESPOONS FLOUR

⅓ CUP CHICKEN BROTH

⅓ CUP RAISINS

¼ TEASPOON BLACK PEPPER

PINCH OF SALT

4 SKINLESS, BONELESS CHICKEN BREAST HALVES (ABOUT 1¼ POUNDS TOTAL)

1. Preheat the oven to 425°.

2. In a medium skillet, warm the oil over medium-high heat. Add the shallots, garlic, carrot, and mushrooms, and cook, stirring frequently, until the mixture begins to brown, 3 to 5 minutes.

3. Add the curry powder and cook, stirring, until fragrant, about 20 seconds. Add the flour and cook, stirring constantly, until the flour is no longer visible, about 30 seconds.

4. Add the broth, raisins, pepper, and salt, and bring to a boil, stirring constantly. Reduce the heat to low, cover, and simmer the curry sauce while you prepare the chicken packets.

5. Cut four 12-inch squares of foil. Place a chicken breast in the center of each square. Dividing evenly, spoon the curry sauce over the chicken. Fold the foil together and seal, then crimp the edges together to seal them. Place the packets on a baking sheet and bake for 20 minutes, or until the chicken is cooked through.

6. Serve the chicken in or out of the packets.

Baked Chicken with Sweet-and-Sour Fruit

SERVES 4

1 TABLESPOON OLIVE OIL
2 TEASPOONS TARRAGON
½ TEASPOON SALT
½ TEASPOON BLACK PEPPER
2½ POUNDS CHICKEN PARTS
2 TABLESPOONS UNSALTED BUTTER
1 SMALL ONION, COARSELY CHOPPED
2 TABLESPOONS FLOUR

1⅓ CUPS CHICKEN BROTH, PREFERABLY REDUCED-SODIUM
2 TABLESPOONS CIDER VINEGAR
2 TEASPOONS BROWN SUGAR
2 PLUMS, CUT INTO ¼-INCH-THICK WEDGES
1 LARGE APPLE, CUT INTO ¼-INCH-THICK WEDGES

1. Preheat the oven to 425°.

2. In a small bowl, combine the oil, 1 teaspoon of the tarragon, the salt, and pepper.

3. Place the chicken in a roasting pan. Brush the chicken with the seasoned oil, and bake for 15 minutes. Reduce the heat to 375° and bake for 25 minutes longer, or until the chicken is cooked through.

4. Meanwhile, in a medium skillet, melt the butter over medium heat. Add the onion and cook until slightly softened, about 4 minutes. Stir in the flour and cook, stirring constantly, until the flour is no longer visible, about 30 seconds. Stir in the broth, vinegar, brown sugar, and remaining 1 teaspoon tarragon. Bring the mixture to a boil, then reduce the heat to low, cover, and simmer while the chicken cooks.

5. About 10 minutes before the chicken is done, increase the heat under the skillet to medium-high and return the sauce to a boil. Reduce the heat to medium, add the plums and apple, and cook until the fruit is just tender, about 7 minutes.

6. Pour the sauce over the chicken in the roasting pan and toss to coat well. Serve hot.

Rosemary-Baked Chicken and Potatoes

SERVES 4

3 TABLESPOONS OLIVE OIL

2 GARLIC CLOVES, MINCED

¼ CUP CHOPPED FRESH ROSEMARY, OR
2½ TEASPOONS DRIED

¼ CUP FINE UNSEASONED DRY BREAD
CRUMBS

¼ CUP GRATED PARMESAN CHEESE

½ TEASPOON BLACK PEPPER

2½ POUNDS CHICKEN PARTS

1 POUND SMALL RED POTATOES

1. Preheat the oven to 425°. Line a broiler pan with foil.

2. In a small bowl, combine the oil, garlic, and 2 tablespoons of the fresh rosemary (or 1 teaspoon of the dried).

3. In another small bowl, combine the bread crumbs, Parmesan, pepper, and remaining 2 tablespoons fresh rosemary (or 1½ teaspoons dried).

4. Place the chicken parts, skin-side up, on the prepared broiler pan. Sprinkle the bread crumb-Parmesan mixture over the chicken.

5. If the potatoes are very small, leave them whole; otherwise, halve them. Place the potatoes around the chicken.

6. Drizzle the rosemary oil over the chicken and potatoes and bake for 20 minutes.

7. Reduce the oven temperature to 375° and continue baking for 30 to 40 minutes, or until the potatoes are tender and the chicken is golden and cooked through.

PEPPER-PECAN CHICKEN

SERVES 4

2½ POUNDS CHICKEN PARTS

½ CUP BUTTERMILK OR PLAIN LOW-FAT
YOGURT

2 GARLIC CLOVES

½ CUP PECAN HALVES OR PIECES

⅓ CUP FINE UNSEASONED DRY BREAD
CRUMBS

3 TABLESPOONS COLD UNSALTED
BUTTER, CUT INTO PIECES

½ TEASPOON SALT

½ TEASPOON BLACK PEPPER

PINCH OF CAYENNE PEPPER

2 TABLESPOONS HONEY

1. Preheat the oven to 425°. Line a broiler pan with foil.

2. In a large bowl, toss the chicken with the buttermilk until evenly coated and set aside.

3. In a food processor, process the garlic until minced. Add the pecans and process until coarsely chopped. Add the bread crumbs, butter, salt, and black and cayenne peppers. Pulse on and off just to incorporate the butter. Transfer the pecan-bread crumb mixture to a shallow bowl.

4. Drain the chicken parts and dredge them in the pecan-bread crumb mixture. Place the chicken, skin-side up, on the prepared pan. Drizzle the honey over the chicken and bake for 15 minutes.

5. Reduce the oven temperature to 375°. Bake for 25 minutes longer, or until the chicken is crisp and cooked through.

SWEET AFTERTHOUGHT: *For a unique and easy dessert, dissolve 2 packages of fruit-flavored gelatin in 1 cup of hot water. Add 3 ice cubes to cool. Stir in 1 pint of semisoft vanilla ice cream or frozen yogurt and beat with an electric mixer until light and frothy. Cover and place in the freezer to firm up.*

Jamaican Jerk Chicken

SERVES 4

1 FRESH OR PICKLED JALAPEÑO PEPPER

4 GARLIC CLOVES, PEELED

4 QUARTER-SIZE SLICES FRESH GINGER

¼ CUP (PACKED) PARSLEY SPRIGS
   (OPTIONAL)

2 TEASPOONS BASIL

1 TEASPOON CINNAMON

½ TEASPOON SALT

½ TEASPOON ALLSPICE

½ TEASPOON BLACK PEPPER

3 TABLESPOONS YELLOW MUSTARD

2 TABLESPOONS FRESH LIME JUICE

2 TABLESPOONS RED WINE VINEGAR OR
   CIDER VINEGAR

1 TABLESPOON VEGETABLE OIL

1 TEASPOON DARK BROWN SUGAR

2½ POUNDS CHICKEN PARTS

1. Preheat the oven to 375°. Line a broiler pan with foil.

2. If desired, remove the seeds from the jalapeño. In a food processor, combine the jalapeño, garlic, ginger, parsley (if using), basil, cinnamon, salt, allspice, and black pepper, and process until finely chopped. Add the mustard, lime juice, vinegar, oil, and brown sugar, and process until puréed.

3. Place the chicken in a large bowl, add the spice mixture and toss to coat the chicken well. Place the chicken, skin-side up, on the prepared pan and bake for 35 minutes.

4. Remove the chicken from the oven and preheat the broiler. Broil the chicken 4 inches from the heat for 2 to 5 minutes, or until well browned and cooked through.

KITCHEN NOTE: *In the Caribbean, the spice pastes that are used to "jerk" meat and poultry are usually very hot. This version has been toned down, but if you want even less spice, use half a pickled jalapeño pepper in place of a whole fresh one.*

Baked Lime-Ginger Chicken with Garlic Rice

SERVES 4

3 TABLESPOONS FRESH LIME JUICE

1 TABLESPOON GRATED LIME ZEST

½ TEASPOON SALT

½ TEASPOON BLACK PEPPER

¼ TEASPOON RED PEPPER FLAKES

2½ POUNDS CHICKEN PARTS

2 TABLESPOONS OLIVE OIL

2 TABLESPOONS UNSALTED BUTTER

6 GARLIC CLOVES, MINCED

5 QUARTER-SIZE SLICES FRESH GINGER, MINCED

1¼ CUPS FINE UNSEASONED DRY BREAD CRUMBS

1 CUP RICE

2 CUPS CHICKEN BROTH, PREFERABLY REDUCED-SODIUM

1. Preheat the oven to 375°. Line a broiler pan with foil.

2. In a large shallow dish, combine the lime juice, lime zest, salt, black pepper, and red pepper flakes. Add the chicken and toss to coat well with the marinade.

3. In a medium saucepan, warm the oil with the butter over medium heat until the butter is melted. Add the garlic and ginger, and cook, stirring frequently, until very fragrant, about 5 minutes. Remove from the heat and set aside.

4. Place the bread crumbs in a large shallow dish. Roll the chicken parts in the bread crumbs until evenly coated and place them on the prepared pan. Drizzle the chicken with 3 tablespoons of the garlic-ginger mixture and bake for 45 minutes, or until the chicken is cooked through.

5. Meanwhile, return the saucepan with the remaining garlic-ginger mixture to medium-high heat. Add the rice and sauté until the rice is lightly coated with the oil, 1 to 2 minutes. Add the broth and bring to a boil. Reduce the heat to medium-low, cover, and simmer until the rice is tender and all the liquid is absorbed, about 20 minutes.

6. When the chicken is done, pour any pan juices from the broiler pan into the cooked rice. Serve the chicken over the rice.

Quick Curry-Roasted Chicken

SERVES 4

ONE 2½- TO 3-POUND CHICKEN
¾ TEASPOON CURRY POWDER
½ TEASPOON SALT

1 TABLESPOON OLIVE OIL
¼ TEASPOON BLACK PEPPER

1. Preheat the oven to 425°.

2. Lay the chicken breast-side down on a work surface. With poultry shears, cut the chicken from back to front along one side of the backbone. Repeat the process on the other side of the backbone; discard the bone. Turn the chicken breast-side up and flatten with the heel of your hand. Cut off the wing tips.

3. In a small bowl, blend the curry powder and salt. Rub the chicken, inside and out, with 1½ teaspoons of the oil. Add the remaining 1½ teaspoons oil to the curry powder mixture and stir to make a paste. Rub the paste on both sides of the chicken. Sprinkle with the pepper.

4. Place the chicken on a rack in a roasting pan, skin-side up. Tuck the wings underneath. Roast the chicken for 45 to 55 minutes, or until a leg joint moves freely and the skin is golden.

5. Transfer the chicken to a serving platter and let it rest for 5 to 10 minutes. Cut into quarters and serve.

KITCHEN NOTE: *In order to cut the time it takes to roast a whole chicken, the bird is split at the backbone and flattened (a technique called spatchcocking) and then roasted on a rack. This method allows the oven heat to circulate around the chicken and cook it from both sides instead of from the outside in as with a conventional whole roast chicken recipe.*

CORNISH HENS
WITH SAUSAGE AND VEGETABLES

SERVES 4

TWO 1½-POUND CORNISH HENS
¼ TEASPOON SALT
¼ TEASPOON BLACK PEPPER
4 GARLIC CLOVES—2 LIGHTLY
  CRUSHED AND 2 MINCED
1 TABLESPOON CHOPPED FRESH MINT,
  OR 1 TEASPOON DRIED
3 TABLESPOONS OLIVE OIL

1 CUP DRY SHERRY
2 TABLESPOONS FRESH LEMON JUICE
2 LARGE ONIONS, COARSELY CHOPPED
¾ POUND CHORIZO OR OTHER SPICY
  SAUSAGE, CUT INTO 1-INCH PIECES
1½ CUPS CHICKEN BROTH
2 LARGE CARROTS, HALVED CROSSWISE
1 HEAD CABBAGE, CUT INTO 8 WEDGES

1. Preheat the oven to 400°. Sprinkle the cavities of the hens with the salt and pepper. Place 1 crushed garlic clove and a pinch of mint in each hen. Reserve the remaining mint.

2. In a large nonstick skillet, warm 2 tablespoons of the oil over medium-high heat. Add the hens and sauté until browned on all sides, 5 to 7 minutes. Place the hens breast-side up on a rack in a roasting pan.

3. Add ½ cup of the sherry and the lemon juice to the skillet and boil for 1 minute. Brush the hens all over with this mixture. Pour any remaining basting mixture into a small bowl. Roast the hens for 45 minutes, or until cooked through, basting occasionally.

4. Meanwhile, in the same skillet, warm the remaining 1 tablespoon oil over medium

heat. Add the onions and minced garlic, and cook, stirring, until the onions are translucent, 2 minutes. Add the sausage and brown well, 3 to 5 minutes.

5. Add the broth, the remaining ½ cup sherry, and the remaining mint. Increase the heat to high and bring to a boil. Add the carrots and cabbage, reduce the heat to medium-low, and simmer, covered, until the vegetables are tender, 15 minutes.

6. With a slotted spoon, transfer the cabbage, carrots, and sausage to a bowl. Skim the fat from the cooking liquid and boil until reduced by half, about 8 minutes.

7. Halve the hens and divide them, the sausage, and vegetables among 4 plates. Serve with the braising liquid.

LEMON-STUFFED ROASTED CHICKEN

SERVES 4

4 TABLESPOONS UNSALTED BUTTER,
  MELTED
4 SCALLIONS, COARSELY CHOPPED
3 GARLIC CLOVES, MINCED
3 TEASPOONS BASIL

½ TEASPOON BLACK PEPPER
3 LEMONS
ONE 3-POUND CHICKEN
½ TEASPOON SALT

1. Preheat the oven to 425°.

2. In a small bowl, combine the butter, scallions, garlic, 2 teaspoons of the basil, and ¼ teaspoon of the pepper.

3. Prick 2 of the lemons all over with a fork and then halve them. Cut the third lemon into thin slices.

4. Place the chicken in a roasting pan. Sprinkle the salt and the remaining 1 teaspoon basil and ¼ teaspoon pepper in the cavity of the chicken, then stuff the lemon halves into the cavity.

5. Arrange the lemon slices over the chicken and spoon on some of the scallion-basil butter. Roast the chicken for 15 minutes.

6. Reduce the oven temperature to 350° and roast the chicken for 45 minutes longer, or until the juices run clear; baste every 15 minutes with the remaining scallion-basil butter.

7. Transfer the chicken to a serving platter and let it rest for 5 to 10 minutes before carving. Serve the chicken with some of the pan juices spooned on top.

VARIATION: *Replace one of the lemons with half an orange and use 2 teaspoons of rosemary in place of the basil.*

THYME-ROASTED CHICKEN

SERVES 4

ONE 3½- TO 4-POUND CHICKEN
½ TEASPOON SALT
½ TEASPOON BLACK PEPPER
1 TABLESPOON FRESH THYME LEAVES,
  STEMS RESERVED

6 TO 8 BAY LEAVES, BROKEN INTO
  SMALL PIECES
½ CUP DRY WHITE WINE

1. Season the body cavity of the chicken with ⅛ teaspoon each of the salt and pepper. Working from the edge of the cavity, gently lift the skin covering the breast, taking care not to tear it, and distribute the thyme leaves under the skin so that they evenly cover the meat. Ease the skin back into place. Place the thyme stems and bay leaf pieces in the cavity and truss the chicken.

2. Fill a covered roasting pan ½ inch deep with water. Set a roasting rack in the pan (making sure it holds the chicken above the water) and place the chicken on the rack. Place the roasting pan over high heat, cover tightly, and steam the chicken for 15 minutes to begin to render its fat.

3. Meanwhile, preheat the oven to 400°.

4. Carefully remove the chicken and rack from the pan. Pour the water (and rendered fat) out of the pan and replace the rack and chicken. Season the outside of the chicken with the remaining ⅜ teaspoon each salt and pepper. Place the chicken in the oven and roast for 40 to 45 minutes, or until light golden brown and cooked through.

5. Remove the chicken and pour the contents of its cavity into the roasting pan. Place the chicken on a serving platter and set aside.

6. Add 1 cup of water and the wine to the roasting pan. Place the pan over medium heat and simmer the liquid, scraping up any browned bits from the bottom of the pan, until the liquid is reduced by half, 7 to 10 minutes. Strain the sauce into a sauceboat.

7. Carve the chicken and serve with the sauce.

ROAST CHICKEN WITH BASIL-YOGURT SAUCE

SERVES 4

ONE 3-POUND CHICKEN, CUT INTO
   QUARTERS, WING TIPS DISCARDED
1 CUP PLAIN LOW-FAT YOGURT
1 CUP FRESH BASIL LEAVES, CHOPPED
3 SCALLIONS, CHOPPED

2 GARLIC CLOVES, MINCED
1 TABLESPOON OLIVE OIL
⅓ CUP GRATED PARMESAN CHEESE
¼ TEASPOON BLACK PEPPER
⅛ TEASPOON SALT

1. Fill a covered roasting pan ½ inch deep with water. Set a roasting rack in the pan (making sure it holds the chicken above the water) and place the chicken on the rack. Place the roasting pan over high heat, cover tightly, and steam the chicken for 15 minutes to begin to render its fat.

2. Meanwhile, preheat the oven to 400°.

3. In a food processor or blender, purée the yogurt, basil, scallions, garlic, oil, and half the Parmesan. Set the basil-yogurt sauce aside at room temperature.

4. Carefully remove the chicken and rack from the pan. Pour the water (and rendered fat) out of the pan and replace the rack and chicken. Season the chicken with the pepper and salt. Roast the chicken for about 25 minutes, or until the skin is light brown.

5. Remove the chicken from the oven and sprinkle the remaining Parmesan over it. Return the chicken to the oven and roast for 8 to 10 minutes longer, or until the cheese is golden brown and the chicken is cooked through.

6. Transfer the chicken to a serving platter and let it rest for 5 to 10 minutes before carving. Pass the basil-yogurt sauce separately.

ROASTED CORNISH HENS ORIENTAL-STYLE

SERVES 4

3 TABLESPOONS REDUCED-SODIUM SOY
   SAUCE

3 TABLESPOONS KETCHUP

1 TABLESPOON LIGHT BROWN SUGAR

1½ TEASPOONS ORIENTAL (DARK)
   SESAME OIL

2 GARLIC CLOVES, MINCED

TWO 1½-POUND CORNISH HENS

1. In a small bowl, combine the soy sauce, ketchup, brown sugar, sesame oil, and garlic, and stir until well combined.

2. Place the hens on a rack in a roasting pan. Pour the soy sauce mixture over them, completely coating the outside and cavity of each hen. Set aside to marinate for 10 minutes.

3. Preheat the oven to 375°.

4. Roast the hens, breast-side down, for 25 minutes, basting occasionally. Turn the hens breast-side up and roast for 20 minutes, basting occasionally, or until cooked through.

5. Halve the hens and serve hot.

SWEET AFTERTHOUGHT: *In a small saucepan, make a lemon syrup by heating sugar and lemon juice together until the sugar is dissolved. Sweeten the syrup to taste, but make it a little on the tart side. Prick slices of pound cake with a fork and spoon about 2 teaspoons of the warm lemon syrup over each slice so it soaks in. Dust the top of the cake with confectioners' sugar and serve. For an added touch, toast the cake lightly before putting the syrup on.*

Fruit-Glazed Cornish Hens

SERVES 4

◆ EXTRA-QUICK

TWO 1¼-POUND CORNISH HENS, SPLIT

1 TABLESPOON OLIVE OIL

1 TEASPOON SALT

½ TEASPOON BLACK PEPPER

⅓ CUP FRUIT JAM OR JELLY

1. Preheat the broiler. Line a broiler pan with foil.

2. If the hens are not already split, with a heavy knife, cut through the hens at the backbone. Turn the hens, skin-side down, and cut through the white membrane on either side of the breastbone. Bend the breasts backward until the breastbone breaks, then pull out the breastbone and the attached cartilage. Cut the hen in half.

3. In a small bowl, combine the oil, salt, and pepper. Rub the hen halves all over with the seasoned oil and place them, skin-side up, on the prepared broiler pan. Broil the hens 4 inches from the heat for 15 minutes.

4. Meanwhile, in a small saucepan over low heat, warm the jam (or jelly), stirring frequently, until melted, about 4 minutes.

5. Brush the hens with the jam and broil for 3 to 5 minutes longer, or until the hens are glazed and cooked through. Watch carefully to keep the jam from charring. Serve hot.

Substitution: *For this (or any) Cornish hen recipe, you can use bone-in chicken breast instead. The cooking times will be approximately the same, although the chicken breast will take longer if it weighs significantly more than 10 ounces.*

Grilled Hens with Garlic and Ginger

SERVES 6 TO 8

FOUR 1½-POUND CORNISH HENS
¾ CUP REDUCED-SODIUM SOY SAUCE
3 TABLESPOONS OLIVE OIL
1 TABLESPOON ORIENTAL (DARK)
    SESAME OIL

4 GARLIC CLOVES, MINCED
ONE 3-INCH PIECE FRESH GINGER,
    MINCED

1. With poultry or kitchen shears, remove the backbones from the hens by cutting along each side of the backbone until it is freed. Place the hens on a work surface, skin-side up, spread open, and press the breastbone with the heel of your hand to flatten each hen.

2. In a large glass or stainless steel baking dish, combine the soy sauce, olive oil, sesame oil, garlic, ginger, and ¼ cup of water. Add the hens, cover with plastic wrap, and marinate, turning occasionally, for at least 20 minutes. (If marinating for more than 1 hour, place in the refrigerator.)

3. Preheat the broiler or prepare the grill. Remove the hens from the marinade, reserving the marinade. Place the hens on the broiler or grill rack and cook for about 30 minutes, turning and basting frequently with the reserved marinade, or until the hens are cooked through.

4. Place any remaining marinade in a small saucepan and bring to a boil. Simmer for 1 or 2 minutes.

5. Serve the hens with the warmed marinade as a dipping sauce.

Broiled Chicken with Oriental Salad

SERVES 4

6 QUARTER-SIZE SLICES FRESH GINGER, MINCED

4 GARLIC CLOVES, MINCED

3 SCALLIONS, MINCED

¼ CUP ORIENTAL (DARK) SESAME OIL

¾ TEASPOON BLACK PEPPER

½ TEASPOON SALT

4 LARGE BONE-IN CHICKEN BREAST HALVES (ABOUT 2 POUNDS TOTAL), WITH SKIN INTACT

3 TABLESPOONS CHOPPED CILANTRO

1 TABLESPOON FRESH LEMON JUICE

1 TEASPOON GRATED LEMON ZEST

¼ TEASPOON RED PEPPER FLAKES

PINCH OF SUGAR

2 MEDIUM CARROTS, COARSELY CHOPPED

¼ POUND SNOW PEAS, CUT INTO THIN STRIPS

2 CUPS BEAN SPROUTS

1 TABLESPOON SESAME SEEDS

1. Preheat the broiler. Line a broiler pan with foil.

2. In a small bowl, combine the ginger, garlic, and scallions. Stir in 2 tablespoons of the sesame oil, ½ teaspoon of the black pepper, and ¼ teaspoon of the salt. Set aside 1 teaspoon of the mixture for the salad.

3. Smear one-third of the remaining ginger-scallion mixture under the chicken skin and one-third of it on the skin. Place the chicken, skin-side down, on the prepared broiler pan and rub the remaining ginger-scallion mixture on the bone side. Broil the chicken 4 inches from the heat for 9 minutes. Turn the chicken over and broil for 9 minutes, or until golden and cooked through.

4. Meanwhile, in a medium bowl, combine the reserved 1 teaspoon ginger-scallion mixture with the cilantro, lemon juice, lemon zest, red pepper flakes, sugar, and remaining 2 tablespoons sesame oil, ¼ teaspoon salt, and ¼ teaspoon black pepper. Add the carrots, snow peas, and bean sprouts, and toss to blend.

5. Serve the salad with the hot chicken and sprinkle both with the sesame seeds.

Lemon-Herb Marinated Chicken Breasts

SERVES 4

1 MEDIUM ONION, CUT INTO RINGS
1 LARGE GARLIC CLOVE, MINCED
1 TABLESPOON GRATED LEMON ZEST
½ CUP FRESH LEMON JUICE
⅓ CUP OLIVE OIL
2 SPRIGS FRESH THYME, OR
    ½ TEASPOON DRIED

2 TABLESPOONS CHOPPED FRESH BASIL,
    OR 1 TEASPOON DRIED
½ TEASPOON SALT
½ TEASPOON BLACK PEPPER
4 LARGE BONELESS CHICKEN BREAST
    HALVES (ABOUT 1½ POUNDS
    TOTAL), WITH SKIN

1. In a shallow glass or stainless steel baking pan, combine the onion, garlic, and lemon zest. Stir in the lemon juice, oil, thyme, basil, salt, and pepper until well combined.

2. Add the chicken breasts and turn to coat with the marinade. Leave the breasts, skin-side up, so the cut side sits in the marinade. Cover with plastic wrap and marinate for at least 30 minutes. (If marinating for more than 1 hour, place in the refrigerator.)

3. Preheat the broiler or prepare the grill. Remove the chicken from the marinade, reserving the marinade. Place the chicken on the broiler or grill rack and broil or grill 4 inches from the heat for 15 minutes, turning and basting with the reserved marinade, or until cooked through. Serve hot.

VARIATIONS: *A number of herbs would go well with this lemon-based marinade for chicken. Try tarragon in place of the thyme. Or try rosemary (only 1 sprig of fresh or ½ teaspoon well crumbled dried) instead of thyme, and replace the basil with fresh parsley.*

Cajun-Style Grilled Chicken Breasts

SERVES 4

◆ EXTRA-QUICK

4 BONELESS CHICKEN BREAST HALVES
(ABOUT 1½ POUNDS TOTAL), WITH
SKIN
⅓ CUP FRESH LEMON JUICE
2 TABLESPOONS GARLIC POWDER

2 TABLESPOONS ONION POWDER
2 TEASPOONS BLACK PEPPER
1 TEASPOON OREGANO
1 TEASPOON THYME
½ TEASPOON CAYENNE PEPPER

1. Preheat the broiler or prepare the grill. If broiling, line a broiler pan with foil.

2. Place the chicken in a shallow container. Pour the lemon juice over the chicken, turning it over to completely coat.

3. On a plate, combine the garlic powder, onion powder, black pepper, oregano, thyme, and cayenne. Dredge the chicken in the spice mixture.

4. Place the chicken, skin-side down, on the prepared broiler pan or the grill. Broil or grill 4 inches from the heat for about 4 minutes per side, turning once, or until it is golden brown and the juices run clear when the chicken is pierced with a knife.

KITCHEN NOTE: *Spice blends are a staple of the Cajun kitchen; they are rubbed on meat and fish and stirred into vegetables and soups. Garlic and onion powders are a common ingredient in these flavoring blends, as they combine easily with other ground spices.*

BROILED CHICKEN WITH GARLIC-HERB SAUCE

SERVES 4

4 LARGE BONELESS CHICKEN BREAST
   HALVES (ABOUT 1½ POUNDS
   TOTAL), WITH SKIN
3 TABLESPOONS UNSALTED BUTTER, AT
   ROOM TEMPERATURE
3 GARLIC CLOVES, MINCED

¼ CUP CHOPPED PARSLEY
1½ TEASPOONS CRUMBLED SAGE
¼ TEASPOON BLACK PEPPER
2 TABLESPOONS FLOUR
½ CUP CHICKEN BROTH

1. Preheat the broiler. Line a broiler pan with foil.

2. In a small bowl, combine the butter, garlic, parsley, sage, and pepper.

3. Place the chicken on the prepared broiler pan. Spread each breast half with ½ teaspoon of the garlic-herb butter. Broil 4 inches from the heat for 8 minutes, or until golden.

4. Turn the chicken over and spread each breast half with another ½ teaspoon garlic-herb butter. Broil for 8 minutes, or until the chicken is golden brown and the juices run clear when pierced with a knife.

5. Meanwhile, use your fingers to mix the flour into the remaining garlic-herb butter.

6. In a small saucepan, bring the broth and ¼ cup of water to a boil over medium-high heat. Stir the butter-flour mixture, bit by bit, into the hot broth mixture. Reduce the heat to medium-low and simmer for 1 minute.

7. Remove the chicken from the broiler pan. Pour any juices from the pan into the garlic-herb sauce and stir to combine. Serve the chicken breasts topped with the sauce.

Curry-Broiled Chicken with Raisin Chutney

SERVES 4

◆ EXTRA-QUICK

2 TABLESPOONS VEGETABLE OIL

1 TABLESPOON CURRY POWDER

1 TABLESPOON REDUCED-SODIUM SOY
 SAUCE

2 TEASPOONS ORIENTAL (DARK)
 SESAME OIL

½ TEASPOON GRANULATED SUGAR

½ TEASPOON RED PEPPER FLAKES

¼ TEASPOON BLACK PEPPER

4 BONELESS CHICKEN BREAST HALVES
 (ABOUT 1½ POUNDS TOTAL), WITH
 SKIN

1 SMALL ONION, FINELY CHOPPED

1 CUP RAISINS

3 TABLESPOONS FRESH LEMON JUICE

3 TABLESPOONS DARK BROWN SUGAR

2 TABLESPOONS CIDER VINEGAR

1 GARLIC CLOVE, MINCED

1 TABLESPOON CHOPPED CANDIED
 GINGER OR 2 QUARTER-SIZE SLICES
 FRESH GINGER, MINCED

2 TEASPOONS GRATED LEMON ZEST

1. Preheat the broiler. Line a broiler pan with foil.

2. In a small bowl, combine the vegetable oil, curry powder, soy sauce, sesame oil, granulated sugar, ¼ teaspoon of the red pepper flakes, and the black pepper.

3. Place the chicken on the prepared broiler pan, skin-side down, and broil 4 inches from the heat for 4 minutes. Turn the chicken over, brush with the curry paste, and broil for 7 to 9 minutes, or until the chicken is golden brown and cooked through. If portions of the chicken begin to char, cover them with foil.

4. Meanwhile, in a small saucepan, combine the onion, raisins, lemon juice, brown sugar, vinegar, garlic, ginger, lemon zest, and remaining ¼ teaspoon red pepper flakes. Bring the mixture to a boil over medium-high heat, stirring constantly. Reduce the heat to low, cover, and simmer for 2 minutes.

5. Transfer the raisin mixture to a food processor and process to a purée.

6. Serve the chicken with the chutney on the side.

ROSEMARY CHICKEN
WITH WARM WHITE BEAN SALAD

S E R V E S 4

◇ L O W - F A T

2 MEDIUM ONIONS, CHOPPED

¼ CUP THAWED FROZEN ORANGE JUICE
CONCENTRATE

2 TABLESPOONS TOMATO PASTE

2 TABLESPOONS OLIVE OIL

4 GARLIC CLOVES, MINCED

1¾ TEASPOONS ROSEMARY, CRUMBLED

½ TEASPOON BLACK PEPPER

4 SMALL SKINLESS, BONELESS CHICKEN
BREAST HALVES (ABOUT 1 POUND
TOTAL)

ONE 10-OUNCE PACKAGE FROZEN CUT
GREEN BEANS, THAWED

ONE 19-OUNCE CAN WHITE KIDNEY
BEANS (CANNELLINI), RINSED AND
DRAINED

3 TABLESPOONS RED WINE VINEGAR OR
CIDER VINEGAR

1 TABLESPOON DIJON MUSTARD

3 MEDIUM SCALLIONS, CHOPPED

¼ TEASPOON SALT

1. Preheat the broiler.

2. In a small bowl, combine ¼ cup of the onions, the orange juice concentrate, tomato paste, 1 tablespoon of the oil, half the garlic, 1 teaspoon of the rosemary, and ¼ teaspoon of the pepper.

3. Spoon half the orange juice mixture over the chicken and broil 4 inches from the heat for 6 minutes. Turn the chicken over, top with the remaining orange juice mixture, and broil for 10 minutes longer, or until the chicken is cooked through. Transfer to a plate and cover loosely with foil to keep warm.

4. Meanwhile, in a medium skillet, warm the remaining 1 tablespoon oil over medium-high heat. Add the remaining onions and garlic, and stir-fry until the onions begin to brown, about 4 minutes. Add the green beans and stir-fry until they are crisp-tender, 3 to 4 minutes. Add the beans and stir to warm.

5. Stir the vinegar, mustard, and remaining ¾ teaspoon rosemary into the skillet. Remove from the heat. Stir in the scallions, salt, and remaining ¼ teaspoon pepper. Serve the chicken with the bean salad on the side.

BROILED CHICKEN WITH TOMATO BUTTER

SERVES 4

◆ EXTRA-QUICK

¼ CUP FRESH LEMON JUICE

4 SKINLESS, BONELESS CHICKEN BREAST HALVES (ABOUT 1¼ POUNDS TOTAL)

3 SUN-DRIED (NOT OIL-PACKED) TOMATO HALVES

½ CUP BOILING WATER

2 SCALLIONS, CUT INTO 1-INCH LENGTHS

2 TABLESPOONS UNSALTED BUTTER, AT ROOM TEMPERATURE

2 TEASPOONS GRATED LEMON ZEST

PINCH OF DRY MUSTARD

PINCH OF WHITE PEPPER

PINCH OF RED PEPPER FLAKES

1. Place the lemon juice in a medium bowl. Add the chicken and toss to coat.

2. In a small bowl, combine the sun-dried tomatoes and the boiling water. Let stand until the tomatoes are plumped and softened, about 5 minutes. Drain the tomatoes well.

3. Preheat the broiler. Line a broiler pan with foil.

4. In a food processor, chop the sun-dried tomatoes and the scallions. Add the butter, lemon zest, mustard, pepper, and red pepper flakes, and pulse to combine. Transfer half the tomato butter to a small skillet or saucepan and gently warm until just melted.

5. Meanwhile, scrape the remaining tomato butter onto a sheet of waxed paper and mold into a rough log shape. Roll the butter up in the waxed paper and twist the ends to seal. Refrigerate the butter until serving time.

6. Arrange the chicken on the prepared broiler pan. Lightly brush the chicken with the melted tomato butter. Broil 4 inches from the heat for 6 minutes. Turn the chicken over and broil for 6 minutes longer, or until golden brown and cooked through.

7. Cut the cold tomato butter into 8 slices and place 2 slices on each serving of the hot chicken.

Chicken with Citrus-Butter Sauce

SERVES 4

3 TABLESPOONS FRESH LEMON JUICE

2 GARLIC CLOVES, MINCED

1 TABLESPOON OLIVE OIL

2 TEASPOONS GRATED LEMON ZEST

½ TEASPOON BLACK PEPPER

4 SKINLESS, BONELESS CHICKEN BREAST
HALVES (ABOUT 1¼ POUNDS TOTAL)

½ CUP GRAPEFRUIT JUICE

¼ CUP THAWED FROZEN ORANGE JUICE
CONCENTRATE

1 TEASPOON SUGAR

1 LARGE RED ONION, THINLY SLICED

1 TABLESPOON UNSALTED BUTTER, AT
ROOM TEMPERATURE

1 TABLESPOON FLOUR

1 SMALL ORANGE (OR ½ SMALL PINK
GRAPEFRUIT), PEELED AND COARSELY
CHOPPED

2 TEASPOONS GRATED ORANGE ZEST

¼ TEASPOON SALT

1. In a heavy-duty plastic bag, combine 2 tablespoons of the lemon juice, the garlic, oil, 1 teaspoon of the lemon zest, and ¼ teaspoon of the pepper. Add the chicken and toss to coat. Set aside to marinate for 20 minutes.

2. Meanwhile, in a medium saucepan, bring the grapefruit juice, orange juice concentrate, and remaining 1 tablespoon lemon juice to a boil over medium-high heat. Stir in the sugar, reduce the heat to medium, and simmer for 20 minutes to concentrate the mixture.

3. Preheat the broiler. Line a broiler pan with foil. Place the onion slices on the prepared broiler pan. Remove the chicken breasts from the marinade and place them on the onions. Broil 4 inches from the heat for 5 minutes.

4. Turn the chicken over and broil for 7 minutes, or until cooked through. Remove the chicken and onions to a plate and cover loosely. Pour the juices from the broiler pan into the sauce in the saucepan and return the mixture to a simmer over medium-high heat.

5. Meanwhile, with your fingers, thoroughly blend the butter and flour. Add small pieces of the butter-flour mixture to the simmering citrus sauce, stirring well after each addition. Stir in the chopped orange (or grapefruit), orange zest, remaining 1 teaspoon lemon zest, the salt, and remaining ¼ teaspoon pepper.

6. Serve the chicken and broiled onions with the citrus-butter sauce.

Honey-Soy Chicken with Ginger-Carrot Rice Salad

SERVES 4

◇ LOW-FAT

¾ CUP RICE

¼ CUP REDUCED-SODIUM SOY SAUCE

3 GARLIC CLOVES, MINCED

3 QUARTER-SIZE SLICES FRESH GINGER,
  PLUS 2 TEASPOONS GRATED GINGER

1 TABLESPOON HONEY

¼ TEASPOON BLACK PEPPER

1¼ POUNDS SKINLESS, BONELESS
  CHICKEN BREASTS, CUT LENGTHWISE
  INTO THIN STRIPS

2 MEDIUM CARROTS, SHREDDED

¼ CUP CHOPPED CILANTRO

2 TABLESPOONS RICE WINE VINEGAR OR
  DISTILLED WHITE VINEGAR

1 TABLESPOON ORIENTAL (DARK)
  SESAME OIL

1 TEASPOON SESAME SEEDS, TOASTED

1. In a medium saucepan, combine the rice and 1½ cups of water and bring to a boil over high heat. Reduce the heat to medium-low, cover, and simmer until the rice is tender and all the liquid is absorbed, about 20 minutes. Transfer the rice to a large bowl, fluff with a fork, and set aside to cool slightly.

2. Meanwhile, in a shallow bowl, combine 3 tablespoons of the soy sauce, the garlic, ginger slices, honey, and pepper. Add the chicken, toss to coat well, and let stand for 15 minutes.

3. Preheat the broiler.

4. Remove the chicken strips from the marinade. Dividing evenly, thread the chicken onto skewers, and place them on a broiler pan. Broil the chicken 4 inches from the heat for 4 minutes. Turn the skewers over and broil for 4 minutes, or until the chicken is golden and cooked through.

5. Meanwhile, add the carrots, cilantro, grated ginger, vinegar, sesame oil, and remaining 1 tablespoon soy sauce to the cooked rice. Toss gently to combine. When the chicken is done, pour any cooking juices from the broiler pan into the rice salad.

6. Serve the broiled chicken on top of the rice salad. Sprinkle both with the toasted sesame seeds.

BROILED CHICKEN WITH CHEDDAR-DILL SAUCE

SERVES 4

♦ EXTRA-QUICK

3 TABLESPOONS UNSALTED BUTTER
½ CUP FINELY CHOPPED CHIVES OR
   SCALLION GREENS
2 GARLIC CLOVES, MINCED
¼ TEASPOON BLACK PEPPER
4 SKINLESS, BONELESS CHICKEN BREAST
   HALVES (ABOUT 1¼ POUNDS TOTAL)

1½ TABLESPOONS FLOUR
½ CUP LOW-FAT MILK
½ CUP SHREDDED CHEDDAR CHEESE
1½ TABLESPOONS MINCED FRESH DILL,
   OR 1 TEASPOON DRIED
PINCH OF SALT
PINCH OF WHITE PEPPER

1. Preheat the broiler. Line a broiler pan with foil.

2. In a small saucepan, melt 2 tablespoons of the butter. Stir in half of the chives, the garlic, and black pepper. Remove from the heat.

3. Place the chicken on the prepared broiler pan and brush with half of the herbed butter. Broil 4 inches from the heat for 7 minutes. Turn the chicken over, brush with the remaining herbed butter, and broil for 7 minutes, or until the chicken is golden and cooked through.

4. Meanwhile, in a small saucepan, melt the remaining 1 tablespoon butter over medium heat. Stir in the flour and cook, stirring con- stantly, until the flour is no longer visible, about 30 seconds. Gradually stir in the milk and cook, stirring constantly, until smooth. Bring the mixture to a boil.

5. Reduce the heat to medium-low and stir in the Cheddar, dill, remaining chives, salt, and white pepper. Stir until the cheese is melted and remove from the heat. When the chicken is done, pour any juices from the broiler pan into the cheese sauce.

6. Serve the chicken topped with the sauce.

Chicken Breasts with Red Pepper Purée

SERVES 4

2 TABLESPOONS FRESH LEMON JUICE

1 TABLESPOON OLIVE OIL

1 TEASPOON THYME

¼ TEASPOON BLACK PEPPER

4 SKINLESS, BONELESS CHICKEN BREAST
   HALVES (ABOUT 1¼ POUNDS TOTAL)

2 TABLESPOONS UNSALTED BUTTER

1 MEDIUM ONION, COARSELY CHOPPED

2 GARLIC CLOVES, MINCED

1 LARGE RED BELL PEPPER, CUT INTO
   BITE-SIZE PIECES

2 TEASPOONS TOMATO PASTE

1½ TEASPOONS GRATED LEMON ZEST

¼ TEASPOON SALT

1. Preheat the broiler. Line a broiler pan with foil.

2. In a medium bowl, combine 1 tablespoon of the lemon juice, the oil, ½ teaspoon of the thyme, and the black pepper. Add the chicken breasts and turn to coat thoroughly. Set aside.

3. In a small saucepan, warm the butter over medium-high heat until it is melted. Add the onion and garlic and cook, stirring frequently, until the onion is translucent, 2 to 3 minutes.

4. Add the bell pepper, the remaining 1 tablespoon lemon juice, the tomato paste, lemon zest, the remaining ½ teaspoon thyme, and the salt. Reduce the heat to low, cover, and cook until the peppers are softened, about 12 minutes.

5. Meanwhile, place the chicken on the prepared broiler pan and broil 4 inches from the heat for 7 minutes. Turn the chicken over and broil for 7 minutes, or until golden brown and cooked through.

6. Transfer the contents of the saucepan to a food processor or blender and purée. Dividing evenly, spoon the red pepper purée onto 4 plates and place 1 chicken breast on top of each portion. If desired, slice each chicken breast crosswise before serving.

PINEAPPLE-GRILLED CHICKEN BREASTS WITH SALSA

SERVES 4

◇ LOW-FAT

8 MEDIUM SHALLOTS OR 2 SMALL
   ONIONS
4 QUARTER-SIZE SLICES FRESH GINGER
2 GARLIC CLOVES
1 SMALL FRESH OR PICKLED JALAPEÑO
   PEPPER, SEEDED
⅓ CUP (PACKED) CILANTRO SPRIGS
ONE 8-OUNCE CAN JUICE-PACKED
   CRUSHED PINEAPPLE

⅓ CUP PLAIN LOW-FAT YOGURT
3 TABLESPOONS FRESH LEMON JUICE
½ TEASPOON SALT
½ TEASPOON BLACK PEPPER
4 SKINLESS, BONELESS CHICKEN BREAST
   HALVES (ABOUT 1¼ POUNDS TOTAL)
2 TEASPOONS HONEY
2 TEASPOONS GRATED LEMON ZEST

1. Preheat the broiler or prepare the grill. If broiling, line a broiler pan with foil.

2. In a food processor, finely chop the shallots, ginger, garlic, jalapeño, and cilantro, and set aside.

3. Drain the pineapple, reserving the juice. In a shallow bowl, combine ¼ cup of the pineapple juice, half of the shallot-ginger mixture, the yogurt, 2 tablespoons of the lemon juice, and ¼ teaspoon each of the salt and black pepper. Add the chicken and toss to coat.

4. Place the chicken on the prepared broiler pan or the grill rack. Broil or grill the chicken 4 inches from the heat for 10 minutes. Turn the chicken over and broil or grill for about 10 minutes, or until golden brown and cooked through.

5. Meanwhile, in a medium bowl, combine the remaining pineapple juice, remaining 1 tablespoon lemon juice, the honey, lemon zest, the remaining ¼ teaspoon each salt and black pepper, the remaining shallot-ginger mixture, and the drained pineapple. Stir well to combine.

6. Serve the chicken with the pineapple salsa on the side.

Broiled Chicken Breasts with Lemon Rice

SERVES 4

◇ LOW-FAT

¼ CUP PLUS 3 TABLESPOONS FRESH
   LEMON JUICE

2 TEASPOONS GRATED LEMON ZEST

¼ TEASPOON BLACK PEPPER

1 CUP RICE

2 TABLESPOONS OLIVE OIL

4 SKINLESS, BONELESS CHICKEN BREAST
   HALVES (ABOUT 1¼ POUNDS TOTAL)

1 MEDIUM RED ONION

1 GARLIC CLOVE

¼ CUP (PACKED) CILANTRO OR
   PARSLEY SPRIGS

1 CELERY RIB

ONE 4-INCH LENGTH OF CUCUMBER,
   PEELED AND QUARTERED

2 PLUM TOMATOES, QUARTERED

3 TABLESPOONS RED WINE VINEGAR

1. In a medium saucepan, combine 1¾ cups of water, ¼ cup of the lemon juice, the lemon zest, and pepper. Bring the mixture to a boil over high heat. Add the rice, reduce the heat to medium-low, cover, and simmer until the rice is tender, about 20 minutes.

2. Meanwhile, preheat the broiler.

3. In a small bowl, combine 1 tablespoon of the oil with the remaining 3 tablespoons of lemon juice. Place the chicken on a broiler pan and brush with half the lemon juice-oil mixture. Broil the chicken 4 inches from the heat for 10 minutes.

4. Meanwhile, halve the onion crosswise and cut 4 thin slices, reserving the remaining onion. Turn the chicken over, place 1 onion slice on each chicken breast, and brush with the remaining lemon juice-oil mixture. Broil for 10 minutes longer, or until the chicken is cooked through.

5. Meanwhile, in a food processor, mince the garlic and cilantro. Add the celery and remaining red onion, and pulse to coarsely chop. Add the cucumber and pulse briefly. Add the tomatoes and pulse briefly to coarsely chop but not purée. Remove the chopped vegetables to a bowl and stir in the vinegar and remaining 1 tablespoon oil.

6. Serve the chicken on a bed of rice, with the vegetable relish on the side.

ALMOND PESTO CHICKEN WITH TOMATO-BASIL RELISH

SERVES 4

◆ EXTRA-QUICK

3 GARLIC CLOVES, PEELED
1 CUP (PACKED) FRESH BASIL LEAVES,
　　PLUS 2 TABLESPOONS CHOPPED
　　BASIL
¼ CUP BLANCHED ALMONDS
¼ CUP PLUS 1 TABLESPOON OLIVE OIL
¼ CUP GRATED PARMESAN CHEESE

½ TEASPOON SALT
⅜ TEASPOON BLACK PEPPER
2½ POUNDS CHICKEN PARTS
1 POUND PLUM TOMATOES, COARSELY
　　CHOPPED
2 TABLESPOONS RED WINE VINEGAR OR
　　CIDER VINEGAR

1. Preheat the broiler. Line a broiler pan with foil.

2. In a food processor, finely chop the garlic, the 1 cup basil leaves, and the almonds. Add ¼ cup of the olive oil, the Parmesan, salt, and ¼ teaspoon of the pepper. Process to a purée.

3. Place the chicken, skin-side down, on the prepared broiler pan. Spoon half of the almond pesto over the chicken and broil 4 inches from the heat for 10 minutes. Turn the chicken over, spread with the remaining almond pesto, and broil for 10 minutes, or until the chicken is golden and cooked through.

4. Meanwhile, in a small bowl, combine the tomatoes, vinegar, the 2 tablespoons chopped basil, and the remaining 1 tablespoon oil and ⅛ teaspoon pepper. Stir to blend.

5. Serve the chicken with the tomato-basil relish on the side.

KITCHEN NOTE: *Although this broiled chicken takes under 30 minutes to prepare, you can make it an almost effort-free dish by making the almond pesto and the tomato-basil relish ahead of time. In fact, you could make a double or triple batch of the pesto and freeze it in small containers for use any time.*

Chili-Rubbed Chicken with Corn-Avocado Salad

SERVES 4

½ CUP REDUCED-FAT MAYONNAISE

⅓ CUP FRESH LIME JUICE

¼ CUP CHOPPED PARSLEY (OPTIONAL)

2 GARLIC CLOVES, MINCED

2 TABLESPOONS CHILI POWDER

1 TABLESPOON OLIVE OIL

1 TABLESPOON CUMIN

2 TEASPOONS GRATED LIME ZEST

½ TEASPOON SALT

¼ TEASPOON BLACK PEPPER

4 WHOLE CHICKEN LEGS (DRUMSTICK
    AND THIGH), ABOUT 2¼ POUNDS
    TOTAL

12 CHERRY TOMATOES, HALVED

ONE 10-OUNCE PACKAGE FROZEN
    CORN, THAWED

1 AVOCADO, DICED

2 TABLESPOONS CHOPPED CILANTRO

1. Preheat the broiler. Line a broiler pan with foil and lightly grease the foil.

2. In a serving bowl, combine the mayonnaise, lime juice, parsley (if using), garlic, chili powder, oil, cumin, lime zest, salt, and pepper. Measure out ¼ cup of the chili mayonnaise to rub on the chicken.

3. Place the chicken legs, skin-side down, on the prepared broiler pan. Coat them with half of the reserved ¼ cup chili mayonnaise. Broil 4 inches from the heat for about 8 minutes, or until the chicken begins to brown.

4. Turn the chicken legs over and coat them with the remaining 2 tablespoons chili mayonnaise. Broil for about 8 minutes, or until the chicken is browned and cooked through.

5. Meanwhile, add the tomatoes, corn, and avocado to the chili mayonnaise in the serving bowl. Toss gently to combine, then stir in the cilantro.

6. Serve the hot chicken legs with the corn-avocado salad on the side.

GRILLED ORANGE-CUMIN CHICKEN THIGHS

SERVES 4

◆ EXTRA-QUICK

2 GARLIC CLOVES, MINCED

½ CUP THAWED FROZEN ORANGE JUICE
CONCENTRATE

¼ CUP CHOPPED PARSLEY

2 TABLESPOONS OLIVE OIL

2 TABLESPOONS HONEY

2 TABLESPOONS TOMATO PASTE

1½ TEASPOONS CUMIN

½ TEASPOON SALT

¼ TEASPOON BLACK PEPPER

8 SMALL BONE-IN CHICKEN THIGHS
(ABOUT 1¾ POUNDS TOTAL), WITH
SKIN

1. Preheat the broiler or prepare the grill. If broiling, line a broiler pan with foil.

2. In a large bowl, stir together the garlic, orange juice concentrate, parsley, oil, honey, tomato paste, cumin, salt, and pepper. Add the chicken thighs and toss to coat.

3. Remove the chicken from the marinade, reserving the marinade. Arrange the chicken on the prepared broiler pan or the grill.

4. Broil or grill the chicken 4 inches from the heat for about 10 minutes per side, brushing with the reserved marinade, or until browned on all sides and the juices run clear when the chicken is pierced with a knife.

SWEET AFTERTHOUGHT: *For an easy "ice cream sandwich" pie, crumble enough chocolate sandwich cookies to make 2½ cups of coarse crumbs. Place 1 cup of the crumbs in a pie pan (you don't even have to press them in, just cover the bottom). Spoon ice cream—soft-serve ice cream or frozen yogurt is ideal—over the crumbs and press down to be sure the ice cream adheres to the crumbs. Sprinkle the remaining crumbs over the top and refreeze.*

Chicken Thighs Broiled with Sherry and Honey

SERVES 4

◇ LOW-FAT

1 TABLESPOON CORNSTARCH
1 CUP PLUS 2 TABLESPOONS DRY
  SHERRY
3 TABLESPOONS HONEY
3 TABLESPOONS RED WINE VINEGAR
1 TABLESPOON REDUCED-SODIUM SOY
  SAUCE

4 GARLIC CLOVES, MINCED
¼ TEASPOON SALT
8 SMALL BONE-IN CHICKEN THIGHS
  (ABOUT 1¾ POUNDS TOTAL),
  SKINNED

1. In a small bowl, blend the cornstarch with 2 tablespoons of the sherry. Set aside.

2. In a small saucepan, boil the remaining 1 cup sherry until it is reduced by half, about 7 minutes. Remove the pan from the heat and whisk in the honey, vinegar, soy sauce, and garlic. Return the pan to the heat and whisk in the cornstarch mixture. Bring the sauce to a boil and cook for 1 minute, whisking constantly. Remove the pan from the heat and set aside to cool.

3. Preheat the broiler. Sprinkle the salt on both sides of the chicken thighs and lay them, bone-side up, on a broiler pan. Brush the chicken liberally with the sauce, then broil them 4 to 6 inches from the heat for 6 to 7 minutes. Turn them over and brush them again with some of the sauce. Broil the chicken for 3 to 4 minutes.

4. Brush the chicken again with the remaining sauce and broil for 5 to 7 minutes, or until the juices run clear when a thigh is pierced with the tip of a sharp knife. Transfer the chicken to a platter and pour any cooking juices from the broiler pan over them.

DEVILISH DRUMSTICKS
WITH CHEESE SAUCE

SERVES 4

◆ EXTRA-QUICK

ONE 3-OUNCE PACKAGE NEUFCHÂTEL
   CREAM CHEESE, AT ROOM
   TEMPERATURE
¼ CUP PLAIN LOW-FAT YOGURT
2 TABLESPOONS CHOPPED PARSLEY
1 GARLIC CLOVE, MINCED
½ TEASPOON OREGANO

¼ TEASPOON SALT
¼ TEASPOON BLACK PEPPER
3 TABLESPOONS UNSALTED BUTTER,
   MELTED
3 TABLESPOONS HOT PEPPER SAUCE
8 SMALL CHICKEN DRUMSTICKS (ABOUT
   1¾ POUNDS TOTAL)

1. Preheat the broiler. Line a broiler pan with foil.

2. In a small bowl, mix together the cream cheese, yogurt, parsley, garlic, oregano, salt, and pepper. Cover the bowl and refrigerate until serving time.

3. In a medium bowl, combine the melted butter and the hot pepper sauce and mix well.

4. Dip each drumstick into the butter mixture until completely coated and place on the prepared pan. Broil the drumsticks 4 inches from the heat for 8 minutes. Turn the drumsticks over and broil for about 8 minutes, or until the skin is golden and the juices run clear when pierced with a knife.

5. Serve the drumsticks with the cream cheese sauce on the side.

VARIATION: *For a variation that makes this recipe similar to its inspiration, the Buffalo chicken wing, use a mild, rich blue cheese in place of the cream cheese called for.*

Citrus-Ginger Drumsticks

SERVES 4

5 QUARTER-SIZE SLICES FRESH GINGER, MINCED

4 SCALLIONS, FINELY CHOPPED

2 GARLIC CLOVES, MINCED

½ CUP ORANGE JUICE

2 TABLESPOONS GRATED ORANGE ZEST

2 TABLESPOONS FRESH LIME JUICE

1 TEASPOON GRATED LIME ZEST

3 TABLESPOONS HONEY

1 TABLESPOON OLIVE OIL

½ TEASPOON SALT

¼ TEASPOON BLACK PEPPER

8 CHICKEN DRUMSTICKS (ABOUT 2½ POUNDS TOTAL)

1. In a plastic bag set in a bowl, combine the ginger, scallions, garlic, orange juice, orange zest, lime juice, and lime zest. Add the honey, oil, salt, and pepper. Add the chicken and shake to thoroughly coat.

2. Seal the bag and let the chicken marinate for at least 30 minutes. (If marinating for more than 1 hour, place in the refrigerator.) Turn the bag occasionally to make sure the chicken is well covered with marinade.

3. Preheat the broiler. Line a broiler pan with foil.

4. Remove the chicken from the marinade, reserving the marinade, and arrange the chicken on the prepared broiler pan. Pour the reserved marinade into a small saucepan and bring it to a boil over medium-high heat. Reduce the heat to low, cover, and simmer, stirring occasionally, while you cook the drumsticks.

5. Broil the chicken 4 inches from the heat for 8 minutes. Turn the drumsticks over and brush them with some of the marinade. Broil for 8 minutes longer, or until cooked through.

6. Return any remaining marinade to a boil again and serve hot with the drumsticks.

HONEY-THYME
TURKEY WITH LEMON NOODLES

SERVES 4

◆ EXTRA-QUICK ◇ LOW-FAT

2 TABLESPOONS PLUS 1 TEASPOON
UNSALTED BUTTER

2 TABLESPOONS HONEY

1 TEASPOON THYME

½ TEASPOON SALT

½ TEASPOON BLACK PEPPER

4 TURKEY CUTLETS (ABOUT 1 POUND
TOTAL)

¾ POUND WIDE EGG NOODLES

3 SCALLIONS, COARSELY CHOPPED

3 TABLESPOONS FRESH LEMON JUICE

1½ TEASPOONS GRATED LEMON ZEST

1. Preheat the broiler. Line a broiler pan with foil and lightly grease the foil.

2. In a small saucepan, combine 2 tablespoons of the butter, the honey, thyme, and ¼ teaspoon each salt and pepper. Cook over low heat until the butter is melted.

3. Place the turkey cutlets on the prepared broiler pan. Brush them with half the honey-butter mixture and broil 4 inches from the heat for about 4 minutes, or until lightly browned. Turn the cutlets over, brush with the remaining honey-butter mixture, and broil for 3 minutes, or until cooked through.

4. Meanwhile, in a large pot of boiling water, cook the noodles until al dente according to package directions.

5. Drain the noodles and place them in a medium bowl. Add the scallions, the remaining 1 teaspoon butter, ¼ teaspoon salt, and ¼ teaspoon pepper, the lemon juice, lemon zest, and any juices from the broiler pan. Toss well to coat. Serve the lemon noodles with the turkey.

GINGERED TURKEY KEBABS

SERVES 4

◆ EXTRA-QUICK ◇ LOW-FAT

3 TEASPOONS MINCED FRESH GINGER

2 GARLIC CLOVES, MINCED

¼ CUP REDUCED-SODIUM SOY SAUCE

1 TABLESPOON ORIENTAL (DARK) SESAME OIL

2 TEASPOONS CIDER VINEGAR

½ TEASPOON HONEY

¼ TEASPOON WHITE PEPPER

¾ POUND TURKEY CUTLETS, CUT LENGTHWISE INTO 1-INCH-WIDE STRIPS

24 CHERRY TOMATOES

1 MEDIUM ZUCCHINI, HALVED LENGTHWISE AND CUT CROSSWISE INTO 1-INCH CHUNKS

1 LARGE RED BELL PEPPER, CUT INTO 1-INCH SQUARES

1 TEASPOON SESAME SEEDS

1. In a shallow dish, combine the ginger, garlic, soy sauce, sesame oil, vinegar, honey, and white pepper. Add the turkey strips to the marinade and stir to coat them thoroughly.

2. Preheat the broiler. Line a broiler pan with foil.

3. Remove the turkey strips from the marinade, reserving the marinade. Dividing the ingredients evenly among 12 skewers, weave the turkey strips around the cherry tomatoes, zucchini, and bell pepper.

4. Place the skewers on the prepared broiler pan and brush them with the reserved marinade. Sprinkle them with sesame seeds and broil 4 inches from the heat for 3 minutes. Turn the kebabs over and broil for about 3 minutes, or until the turkey is lightly browned and cooked through.

GLAZED CHICKEN KEBABS WITH PINEAPPLE

SERVES 4

◆ EXTRA - QUICK ◇ LOW - FAT

ONE 20-OUNCE CAN JUICE-PACKED
PINEAPPLE CHUNKS

2 TABLESPOONS CIDER VINEGAR

2 TABLESPOONS LIGHT BROWN SUGAR

1 TABLESPOON CORNSTARCH

½ TEASPOON GROUND GINGER

½ TEASPOON SALT

2 POUNDS SKINLESS, BONELESS
CHICKEN BREASTS, CUT INTO
1-INCH CHUNKS

2 MEDIUM GREEN BELL PEPPERS, CUT
INTO 1-INCH SQUARES

1. Drain the pineapple, reserving 1 cup of the juice. Set the pineapple chunks aside.

2. In a small saucepan, combine the reserved pineapple juice, the vinegar, brown sugar, cornstarch, ginger, and salt, and stir to blend. Cook the mixture over medium heat, stirring constantly, until it thickens, about 2 minutes. Remove the pan from the heat and set aside.

3. Preheat the broiler or prepare the grill. If broiling, line a baking sheet with foil.

4. Dividing the ingredients evenly, thread the chicken chunks, bell pepper squares, and pineapple chunks alternately on 8 to 12 skew-

ers. Brush the kebabs generously with the pineapple sauce. If broiling, place the kebabs on the baking sheet before brushing them.

5. Broil or grill the kebabs 4 inches from the heat for 2 to 3 minutes, or until the chicken begins to brown. Turn the kebabs, brush them with the remaining pineapple sauce, and broil or grill for 2 to 3 minutes, or until the chicken is cooked through.

Chicken and Tomatoes with Lemon Vinaigrette

SERVES 4

◆ EXTRA-QUICK

2 GARLIC CLOVES
⅓ CUP FRESH BASIL LEAVES, OR
   2 TEASPOONS DRIED
1½ TEASPOONS FRESH THYME, OR
   ½ TEASPOON DRIED
¼ CUP OLIVE OIL

¼ CUP FRESH LEMON JUICE
2 TEASPOONS GRATED LEMON ZEST
4 SKINLESS, BONELESS CHICKEN BREAST
   HALVES (ABOUT 1¼ POUNDS TOTAL)
3 MEDIUM PLUM TOMATOES, SLICED

1. Preheat the broiler. Line a broiler pan with foil.

2. In a food processor, mince the garlic. Add the basil and thyme, and finely mince. Add the oil, lemon juice, and lemon zest, and pulse until blended. Measure out 3 tablespoons of this mixture to use as a basting mixture for the chicken.

3. Place the chicken on the prepared broiler pan and brush with 1 tablespoon of the reserved basting mixture. Broil the chicken 4 inches from the heat for 10 minutes, or until it begins to brown.

4. Meanwhile, place the tomatoes in a shallow bowl and pour the mixture remaining in the food processor over them; set aside.

5. Turn the chicken over and brush with the remaining 2 tablespoons basting mixture. Broil 4 inches from the heat for 6 minutes, or until the chicken is browned and cooked through.

6. To serve, slice the chicken across the grain on the diagonal. Serve with the tomatoes and spoon some of the vinaigrette on top.

CHICKEN BREASTS
WITH TOMATO-BASIL MAYONNAISE

SERVES 4

2 PLUM TOMATOES, SEEDED AND DICED
½ TEASPOON SALT
1 CUP DRY WHITE WINE (OPTIONAL)
½ CUP CHOPPED CELERY LEAVES
10 SPRIGS PARSLEY
2 SCALLIONS, SPLIT LENGTHWISE
¼ TEASPOON WHITE OR BLACK
   PEPPERCORNS

4 SKINLESS, BONELESS CHICKEN BREAST
   HALVES (ABOUT 1¼ POUNDS TOTAL)
⅔ CUP REDUCED-FAT MAYONNAISE
2 TABLESPOONS CHOPPED FRESH BASIL,
   OR 2 TEASPOONS DRIED
1 TEASPOON FRESH LEMON JUICE
¼ TEASPOON CAYENNE PEPPER
2 MEDIUM TOMATOES, SLICED

1. Place the diced tomatoes in a colander and sprinkle with the salt. Set aside to drain while you cook the chicken.

2. In a large saucepan, bring 2 quarts of water, the wine (if using), celery leaves, parsley, scallions, and peppercorns to a boil over medium-high heat. Add the chicken, reduce the heat to low, and simmer gently until the chicken is just cooked through, about 20 minutes. Drain the chicken, discarding the cooking liquid or reserving it for another use. Set the chicken aside to cool.

3. Meanwhile, drain the diced tomatoes on paper towels to remove excess moisture, and place them in a small bowl. Add the mayonnaise and stir to mix, crushing some of the tomatoes slightly with a fork. Stir in the basil, lemon juice, and cayenne.

4. When the chicken is cool enough to handle, cut it lengthwise into ¼-inch-wide slices. Arrange the slices, slightly overlapping, on a large platter. Spread the tomato-basil mayonnaise over the chicken and surround it with the sliced tomatoes.

Chicken-Cucumber Salad with Tarragon

SERVES 4

♦ EXTRA-QUICK ◊ LOW-FAT

½ CUP CHICKEN BROTH

2 TABLESPOONS MINCED FRESH
    TARRAGON, OR 1½ TEASPOONS
    DRIED

2 GARLIC CLOVES, MINCED

¼ TEASPOON BLACK PEPPER

¾ POUND SKINLESS, BONELESS
    CHICKEN BREASTS, THINLY SLICED
    ACROSS THE GRAIN

⅓ CUP PLAIN LOW-FAT YOGURT

1 TABLESPOON OLIVE OIL

1 TABLESPOON RICE WINE VINEGAR OR
    WHITE WINE VINEGAR

½ TEASPOON SALT

1 MEDIUM CUCUMBER, PEELED AND
    CUBED

1 LARGE RED BELL PEPPER, COARSELY
    CHOPPED

1. In a medium saucepan, combine the broth, half the tarragon, the garlic, and black pepper. Bring to a boil over medium-high heat. Add the chicken slices and return to a boil. Reduce the heat to low, cover, and simmer, stirring occasionally, until the chicken is cooked through, about 7 minutes.

2. Meanwhile, in a small bowl, combine the yogurt, oil, vinegar, salt, and remaining tarragon, and stir to blend.

3. With a slotted spoon, transfer the chicken to a large bowl (reserve the broth for another use or discard). Add the cucumber, bell pepper, and yogurt dressing, and toss to combine.

4. Line 4 serving plates with the lettuce leaves and spoon the chicken salad on top.

FRENCH POTATO-CHICKEN SALAD

SERVES 4

1 POUND UNPEELED RED POTATOES, CUT INTO ½-INCH CHUNKS

ONE 10-OUNCE PACKAGE FROZEN CUT GREEN BEANS, THAWED

½ POUND SKINLESS, BONELESS CHICKEN BREASTS, CUT INTO BITE-SIZE PIECES

¼ CUP OLIVE OIL

2 TABLESPOONS WHITE WINE VINEGAR OR CIDER VINEGAR

2 TABLESPOONS MINCED FRESH DILL, OR 2 TEASPOONS DRIED

1 TABLESPOON DIJON MUSTARD

¾ TEASPOON WORCESTERSHIRE SAUCE

¼ TEASPOON SALT

⅛ TEASPOON BLACK PEPPER

1. Steam the potatoes in a steamer over 1 inch of boiling water, covered, for 12 minutes. Add the beans to the steamer tray, cover again, and cook until the potatoes are just tender and the beans are crisp-tender, about 4 minutes longer.

2. Transfer the potatoes and beans to a large serving bowl. Add the chicken to the steamer, cover, and cook until opaque throughout, about 6 minutes.

3. Meanwhile, in a small bowl, whisk together the oil, vinegar, dill, mustard, Worcestershire sauce, salt, and pepper.

4. Add the chicken to the potatoes and beans. Pour the dressing on top and toss well to combine. Serve the salad warm or at room temperature.

SUBSTITUTION: *If you have access to a farmstand market or have your own vegetable garden, this salad is especially good made with fresh green beans. Use ½ pound of fresh and cut into 2-inch lengths. Steam as directed in Step 1 above.*

Chicken Salad with Sesame-Ginger Dressing

SERVES 4

◆ EXTRA-QUICK ◇ LOW-FAT

¾ POUND SKINLESS, BONELESS
   CHICKEN BREASTS
⅓ CUP RICE WINE VINEGAR OR WHITE
   WINE VINEGAR
¼ CUP CHICKEN BROTH
1 TABLESPOON ORIENTAL (DARK)
   SESAME OIL
1 TABLESPOON DIJON MUSTARD
1 TEASPOON REDUCED-SODIUM SOY
   SAUCE
2 GARLIC CLOVES, MINCED

2 QUARTER-SIZE SLICES FRESH GINGER,
   MINCED
3 SCALLIONS, COARSELY CHOPPED
2 MEDIUM CARROTS, THINLY SLICED
1 LARGE RED BELL PEPPER, CUT INTO
   BITE-SIZE PIECES
ONE 8-OUNCE CAN SLICED BAMBOO
   SHOOTS, DRAINED
8 RED LEAF OR ROMAINE LETTUCE
   LEAVES, TORN INTO PIECES

1. Place the chicken in a steamer tray over 1 inch of water, cover, and bring the water to a boil. Reduce the heat to medium-low and cook until the chicken is just cooked through, about 8 minutes. Transfer the chicken to a plate, cover loosely with foil, and let stand for a few minutes.

2. Meanwhile, in a small bowl, combine the vinegar, broth, sesame oil, mustard, soy sauce, garlic, and ginger. Add any juices that have collected under the chicken and stir well to combine.

3. Cut the chicken across the grain into ¼-inch-thick slices.

4. Pour half the dressing into a skillet and warm it over medium heat. Add the scallions and cook until they start to wilt, about 1 minute. Add the carrots, bell pepper, bamboo shoots, and chicken, and cook, stirring, until just heated through, about 3 minutes.

5. In a large serving bowl, toss the chicken mixture with the lettuce and the remaining dressing.

Piquant Lemon Chicken Salad

SERVES 4

◇ LOW-FAT

1 POUND SKINLESS, BONELESS CHICKEN
  BREASTS
¼ CUP PLAIN LOW-FAT YOGURT
¼ CUP FRESH LEMON JUICE
2 TABLESPOONS REDUCED-FAT
  MAYONNAISE
2 TEASPOONS GRATED LEMON ZEST
1½ TEASPOONS GROUND CORIANDER
½ TEASPOON SALT
¼ TEASPOON BLACK PEPPER

¼ TEASPOON CAYENNE PEPPER
3 QUARTER-SIZE SLICES FRESH GINGER,
  MINCED
¼ CUP (PACKED) PARSLEY SPRIGS,
  MINCED (OPTIONAL)
4 SCALLIONS, FINELY CHOPPED
1 LARGE CARROT, FINELY CHOPPED
1 LARGE GREEN BELL PEPPER, CUT INTO
  THIN STRIPS
1 PINT CHERRY TOMATOES, HALVED

1. Place the chicken in a steamer tray over 1 inch of water, cover, and bring the water to a boil. Reduce the heat to medium-low and cook until the chicken is just cooked through, about 10 minutes. Transfer the chicken to a plate; cover loosely with foil to keep warm.

2. Meanwhile, in a large serving bowl, combine the yogurt, lemon juice, mayonnaise, lemon zest, coriander, salt, and black and cayenne peppers.

3. Add the ginger, parsley (if using), scallions, carrot, bell pepper, and cherry tomatoes to the lemon-yogurt dressing.

4. Shred the chicken and add it to the vegetable mixture in the bowl. Toss the ingredients to coat with the dressing.

Red Potato, Broccoli, and Turkey Salad

SERVES 4

◇ LOW-FAT

1 POUND SMALL RED POTATOES, CUT INTO ½-INCH CHUNKS

2 TABLESPOONS OLIVE OIL

2 TABLESPOONS FRESH LEMON JUICE

1 TABLESPOON WHITE WINE VINEGAR

1 TEASPOON GRATED LEMON ZEST

½ TEASPOON GRAINY MUSTARD

1 GARLIC CLOVE, MINCED

½ TEASPOON SUGAR

½ TEASPOON BLACK PEPPER

⅛ TEASPOON SALT

2 CUPS SMALL BROCCOLI FLORETS

1 TART APPLE

10 OUNCES COOKED TURKEY BREAST, CUT INTO ½-INCH CUBES

2 MEDIUM CARROTS, JULIENNED

3 SCALLIONS, CUT ON THE DIAGONAL INTO 1-INCH PIECES

1. In a large saucepan of boiling water, cook the potatoes until they are just tender, about 10 minutes.

2. Meanwhile, in a small bowl, whisk together the oil, 1 tablespoon of the lemon juice, the vinegar, lemon zest, mustard, garlic, sugar, pepper, and salt.

3. With a slotted spoon, transfer the potatoes to a large serving bowl (keep the cooking water for blanching the broccoli). While the potatoes are still hot, add the dressing and toss them well. Let the potatoes cool.

4. Meanwhile, return the water to a boil, add the broccoli, and blanch for 2 minutes. Drain, rinse under cold running water, and drain again. Add the broccoli to the potatoes.

5. Quarter and thinly slice the apple and toss the slices with the remaining 1 tablespoon lemon juice. Add the apple slices, turkey cubes, carrots, and scallions to the potatoes. Toss well to combine and serve at once.

Mexican Turkey Salad

SERVES 4

2 MEDIUM CARROTS, DICED

1½ POUNDS COOKED TURKEY BREAST,
CUT INTO THIN STRIPS

ONE SMALL HEAD CABBAGE, SHREDDED

2 BUNCHES CILANTRO, COARSELY
CHOPPED

½ CUP FRESH LIME JUICE

½ CUP OLIVE OIL

1 GARLIC CLOVE, MINCED

½ TEASPOON CAYENNE PEPPER

½ TEASPOON SALT

HOT PEPPER SAUCE

3 CUPS HALVED CHERRY TOMATOES

1. In a small saucepan of boiling water, blanch the carrots for 2 minutes. Drain, rinse under cold running water, and drain again.

2. In a salad bowl, toss together the carrots, turkey, cabbage, and all but 3 tablespoons of the cilantro.

3. In a small bowl, combine the lime juice, oil, garlic, cayenne, and salt, and whisk until blended. Whisk in hot pepper sauce to taste.

4. Pour the dressing over the salad and top with the cherry tomatoes and the remaining 3 tablespoons cilantro.

SWEET AFTERTHOUGHT: *In Mexico, chocolate, coffee, and cinnamon are frequently used together as complementary flavors in savory dishes as well as desserts. Try a Mexican-inspired pudding by flavoring a storebought chocolate pudding with a little bit of coffee liqueur and a pinch or two of cinnamon. Serve the pudding topped with toasted slivered almonds.*

CURRIED TURKEY SALAD

SERVES 4

◆ EXTRA-QUICK

¼ CUP REDUCED-FAT MAYONNAISE

¼ CUP PLAIN LOW-FAT YOGURT

1 TABLESPOON ORANGE MARMALADE,
APRICOT JAM, OR MANGO CHUTNEY
(OPTIONAL)

2 TEASPOONS CURRY POWDER

⅛ TEASPOON SALT

⅛ TEASPOON BLACK PEPPER

½ POUND COOKED TURKEY, CUT INTO
½-INCH CUBES

1 GRANNY SMITH OR OTHER TART
GREEN APPLE, CUT INTO ½-INCH
CUBES

1 CUP SEEDLESS RED GRAPES

½ CUP CHOPPED WALNUTS OR PECANS

1. In a medium serving bowl, combine the mayonnaise, yogurt, marmalade (if using), curry powder, salt, and pepper.

2. Add the turkey, apple, grapes, and walnuts to the dressing and stir until well combined.

KITCHEN NOTE: *Now that fresh whole turkey and turkey breast are available year round (not just in November), many families are roasting this lean poultry just to have on hand for sandwiches—and salads like this one. Of course, you can also use cooked turkey from the deli or supermarket for the salad: To make it easier to cut into cubes, ask for an unsliced ½-inch-thick piece.*

CHICKEN-VEGETABLE SOUP

SERVES 4

1 TABLESPOON VEGETABLE OIL

1 MEDIUM ONION, COARSELY CHOPPED

1 LARGE GARLIC CLOVE, MINCED

1 CUP CHOPPED CELERY

2 LARGE CARROTS, DICED

3 CUPS CHICKEN BROTH

1 POUND BONE-IN CHICKEN BREAST
HALVES

½ CUP DRY WHITE WINE

¼ POUND MUSHROOMS, SLICED

½ POUND SPINACH, STEMMED AND CUT
INTO 1-INCH-WIDE SHREDS

½ POUND ASPARAGUS SPEARS, CUT
ON THE DIAGONAL INTO
1½-INCH PIECES

½ CUP JULIENNE-CUT LEEK OR
SCALLION WHITES

¼ TEASPOON SALT

¼ TEASPOON BLACK PEPPER

1. In a large saucepan, warm the oil over medium-high heat. Add the onion, garlic, celery, and half of the carrots, and cook, stirring occasionally, until the vegetables are tender, 3 to 4 minutes.

2. Add the broth, 2 cups of water, and the chicken, and bring to a boil over medium-high heat. Cover, reduce the heat to low, and simmer for 20 minutes.

3. Remove the chicken from the broth and set it aside to cool. Pour the broth through a large strainer set over a bowl, pressing on the solids with the back of a spoon to extract as much liquid as possible. Discard the solids.

4. Return the broth to the pan. Add the wine and bring to a boil over medium-high heat. Reduce the heat to medium-low, add the mushrooms and the remaining carrots, and simmer, uncovered, for 10 minutes.

5. Meanwhile, remove the skin and bones from the chicken and discard. Cut the chicken on the diagonal into thin strips.

6. Add the chicken, spinach, asparagus, and leek to the broth and simmer for 5 minutes. Stir in the salt and pepper.

7. Ladle the soup into 4 bowls and serve.

Chicken Stroganoff

SERVES 4

¼ CUP FLOUR

½ TEASPOON SALT

¼ TEASPOON BLACK PEPPER

1¼ POUNDS SKINLESS, BONELESS
  CHICKEN BREASTS, CUT INTO
  BITE-SIZE PIECES

2 TABLESPOONS VEGETABLE OIL

1 MEDIUM ONION, CUT INTO WEDGES

½ POUND SMALL MUSHROOMS, HALVED

½ POUND WIDE EGG NOODLES

2 TABLESPOONS UNSALTED BUTTER

1 TABLESPOON DIJON MUSTARD

1 TABLESPOON PAPRIKA

½ CUP CHICKEN BROTH

¼ CUP REDUCED-FAT SOUR CREAM, AT
  ROOM TEMPERATURE

¼ CUP PLAIN LOW-FAT YOGURT, AT
  ROOM TEMPERATURE

1. In a plastic or paper bag, combine the flour, salt, and pepper, and shake to mix. Add the chicken and shake to coat lightly. Remove the chicken; reserve the excess seasoned flour.

2. In a large nonstick skillet, warm 1 tablespoon of the oil over medium heat. Add the onion and mushrooms, and cook, stirring frequently, until the onion is translucent, about 4 minutes. With a slotted spoon, transfer the mixture to a plate.

3. Add the remaining 1 tablespoon oil to the skillet and increase the heat to medium-high. Add the chicken and stir-fry until golden but not cooked through, about 3 minutes. Transfer the chicken to the mushroom mixture and cover to keep warm.

4. Meanwhile, in a large pot of boiling water, cook the noodles until al dente according to package directions.

5. Add the butter to the skillet and melt over medium heat. Stir in the reserved seasoned flour and cook, stirring constantly, until the flour is blended, about 1 minute. Stir in the mustard and paprika. Add the broth.

6. Bring the mixture to a boil. Return the chicken-mushroom mixture to the skillet, reduce the heat to medium-low, cover, and simmer for 5 minutes.

7. Stir in the sour cream and yogurt and cook until heated through, about 2 minutes.

8. Drain the noodles, divide them among 4 plates, and spoon the sauce on top.

TURKEY FRICASSEE
WITH EGG NOODLES

SERVES 4

◇ LOW-FAT

1¾ CUPS CHICKEN BROTH, PREFERABLY
    REDUCED-SODIUM
2 GARLIC CLOVES, MINCED
¾ TEASPOON THYME
½ TEASPOON SALT
½ TEASPOON BLACK PEPPER
1 POUND SKINLESS, BONELESS TURKEY
    BREAST, CUT INTO BITE-SIZE PIECES
½ POUND SMALL MUSHROOMS

1 CUP FROZEN PEARL ONIONS
½ POUND EGG NOODLES
2 TABLESPOONS CORNSTARCH
2 MEDIUM ZUCCHINI, THINLY SLICED
2 MEDIUM YELLOW SQUASH, THINLY
    SLICED
2 EGG YOLKS
¼ CUP LOW-FAT MILK

1. In a medium skillet, bring 1½ cups of the broth, the garlic, thyme, salt, and pepper to a boil over medium-high heat. Add the turkey, mushrooms, and onions. Return the mixture to a boil, reduce the heat to low, cover, and simmer until the turkey is barely cooked, 8 to 10 minutes.

2. In a large pot of boiling water, cook the noodles according to package directions.

3. Meanwhile, in a small bowl, combine the remaining ¼ cup broth with the cornstarch, and stir to blend.

4. Increase the heat under the turkey mixture to medium-high and bring it to a boil. Stir in the cornstarch mixture, zucchini, and yellow squash, and cook, stirring constantly, until the liquid has thickened slightly. Reduce the heat to medium, cover, and simmer until the vegetables are just tender, about 4 minutes.

5. In another small bowl, beat together the egg yolks and milk. Ladle out about ¼ cup of hot broth from the skillet and gradually beat it into the egg-milk mixture to warm it.

6. Add the warmed egg-milk mixture to the skillet. Cook at a bare simmer, stirring frequently, until the fricassee is slightly thickened, about 5 minutes.

7. Drain the noodles and divide them among 4 plates. Spoon the turkey fricassee on top and serve hot.

CHICKEN CACCIATORE

SERVES 4

¼ CUP FLOUR

¼ TEASPOON BLACK PEPPER

2½ POUNDS CHICKEN PARTS

2 TABLESPOONS OLIVE OIL

1 MEDIUM ONION, COARSELY CHOPPED

3 GARLIC CLOVES, MINCED

1½ CUPS CHICKEN BROTH, PREFERABLY
REDUCED-SODIUM

ONE 16-OUNCE CAN CRUSHED
TOMATOES

¼ CUP TOMATO PASTE

1½ TEASPOONS OREGANO

1 BAY LEAF

¼ POUND SMALL MUSHROOMS

1 MEDIUM ZUCCHINI, THINLY SLICED

¼ CUP CHOPPED PARSLEY

1. In a plastic or paper bag, combine the flour and pepper, and shake to combine. Add the chicken and shake to coat lightly. Reserve the excess seasoned flour.

2. In a large flameproof casserole or Dutch oven, warm the oil over medium-high heat. Add the chicken and cook until golden brown on all sides, 6 to 8 minutes. Transfer the chicken to a plate and cover loosely with foil to keep warm.

3. Add the onion and garlic to the casserole and cook until the onion begins to brown, about 5 minutes. Stir in the reserved seasoned flour and cook, stirring constantly, until the flour is no longer visible.

4. Stir in the broth, tomatoes, tomato paste, oregano, and bay leaf. Bring the mixture to a boil. Return the chicken (and any juices that have collected on the plate) to the casserole. Add the mushrooms. Reduce the heat to medium-low, cover, and simmer, turning the chicken occasionally, for 30 minutes.

5. Add the zucchini and cook, uncovered, just until tender, about 5 minutes. Just before serving, remove and discard the bay leaf and stir in the parsley.

TURKEY PARMESAN WITH FRESH TOMATO SAUCE

SERVES 4

◆ EXTRA-QUICK

½ CUP GRATED PARMESAN CHEESE

¼ CUP FINE UNSEASONED DRY BREAD CRUMBS

1¼ TEASPOONS BASIL

½ TEASPOON BLACK PEPPER

½ TEASPOON SALT

1 EGG

4 TURKEY CUTLETS (ABOUT ¾ POUND TOTAL)

2 TABLESPOONS OLIVE OIL

1 MEDIUM ONION, COARSELY CHOPPED

2 GARLIC CLOVES, MINCED

1 POUND PLUM TOMATOES, COARSELY CHOPPED

½ CUP NO-SALT-ADDED TOMATO SAUCE

½ CUP SHREDDED PART-SKIM MOZZARELLA CHEESE

1. In a shallow bowl, combine ¼ cup of the Parmesan, the bread crumbs, ¼ teaspoon of the basil, ¼ teaspoon of the pepper, and the salt. In another shallow bowl, beat the egg. Dip the turkey cutlets in the beaten egg, turning to coat, then dredge them in the bread crumb mixture until evenly coated.

2. In a large skillet, warm 1 tablespoon of the oil over medium-high heat. Add the cutlets and cook until browned all over, about 3 minutes per side. Transfer the turkey to a plate and cover loosely with foil to keep warm.

3. Add the remaining 1 tablespoon oil to the skillet. Add the onion and garlic, and cook, stirring frequently, for 3 minutes.

4. Add the chopped tomatoes, tomato sauce, the remaining 1 teaspoon basil, and the remaining ¼ teaspoon pepper. Bring the sauce to a boil.

5. Return the turkey (and any juices that have collected on the plate) to the skillet and sprinkle with the mozzarella and the remaining ¼ cup Parmesan. Reduce the heat to medium-low, cover, and simmer until the cheese is melted, about 3 minutes. Serve hot.

HUSHPUPPY CHICKEN BREASTS WITH CORN SALAD

SERVES 4

◆ EXTRA-QUICK ◇ LOW-FAT

3 TABLESPOONS YELLOW CORNMEAL

2 TABLESPOONS FLOUR

1 TEASPOON SALT

½ TEASPOON BLACK PEPPER

PINCH OF CAYENNE PEPPER

4 SKINLESS, BONELESS CHICKEN BREAST
HALVES (ABOUT 1¼ POUNDS
TOTAL), POUNDED ½ INCH THICK

1 TABLESPOON OLIVE OIL

1 TABLESPOON UNSALTED BUTTER

3 TABLESPOONS CIDER VINEGAR

2 TEASPOONS DIJON MUSTARD

¼ TEASPOON SUGAR

3 SCALLIONS, COARSELY CHOPPED

1 MEDIUM RED BELL PEPPER, COARSELY
CHOPPED

ONE 10-OUNCE PACKAGE FROZEN
CORN, THAWED AND DRAINED ON
PAPER TOWELS

¼ CUP CHOPPED PARSLEY (OPTIONAL)

1. In a plastic or paper bag, combine the cornmeal, flour, salt, black pepper, and cayenne, and shake to mix. Add the chicken and shake to coat lightly.

2. In a large skillet, warm the oil with the butter over medium-high heat until the butter is melted. Add the chicken and cook until browned all over and cooked through, about 5 minutes per side.

3. Meanwhile, in a medium bowl, combine the vinegar, mustard, and sugar, and stir well. Add the scallions, bell pepper, and corn, and toss to coat. Add 2 tablespoons of the parsley (if using) and toss again.

4. Serve the chicken garnished with the remaining 2 tablespoons parsley and with the corn salad on the side.

Fried Chicken Strips with Honey Mustard

SERVES 4

◆ EXTRA-QUICK

⅓ CUP FLOUR

2 TABLESPOONS CHOPPED PARSLEY
(OPTIONAL)

1 TEASPOON PAPRIKA

½ TEASPOON SALT

¼ TEASPOON BLACK PEPPER

PINCH OF CAYENNE PEPPER

1¼ POUNDS SKINLESS, BONELESS
CHICKEN BREASTS, CUT ACROSS THE
GRAIN INTO ½-INCH-WIDE STRIPS

2 TABLESPOONS PLUS 1 TEASPOON
VEGETABLE OIL

¼ CUP DIJON MUSTARD OR GRAINY
MUSTARD

1½ TEASPOONS HONEY

1 TEASPOON CIDER VINEGAR

1. In a plastic or paper bag, combine the flour, parsley (if using), paprika, salt, black pepper, and cayenne, and shake to blend. Add the chicken strips and shake to coat lightly.

2. In a large nonstick skillet, warm 2 tablespoons of the oil over medium-high heat. Add the chicken strips in one layer and cook, turning frequently, until golden and just cooked through, about 7 minutes. Drain the chicken on paper towels.

3. In a small bowl, combine the mustard, honey, vinegar, and the remaining 1 teaspoon oil. Stir well to blend.

4. Divide the chicken strips among 4 plates and serve immediately with the honey mustard on the side.

Spicy Chicken-Peanut Stir-Fry

SERVES 4

◆ EXTRA-QUICK

1¼ POUNDS SKINLESS, BONELESS
   CHICKEN BREASTS, CUT INTO BITE-
   SIZE PIECES

2 TABLESPOONS REDUCED-SODIUM SOY
   SAUCE

2 TEASPOONS ORIENTAL (DARK)
   SESAME OIL

3 TEASPOONS CORNSTARCH

⅔ CUP CHICKEN BROTH, PREFERABLY
   REDUCED-SODIUM

2 DROPS HOT PEPPER SAUCE

2 TABLESPOONS OLIVE OIL

8 SCALLIONS, CUT ON THE DIAGONAL
   INTO 2-INCH LENGTHS

2 CELERY RIBS, CUT ON THE DIAGONAL
   INTO ½-INCH PIECES

1 LARGE RED OR GREEN BELL PEPPER,
   CUT INTO BITE-SIZE PIECES

3 QUARTER-SIZE SLICES FRESH GINGER,
   SLIVERED

3 GARLIC CLOVES, MINCED

½ CUP UNSALTED PEANUTS

¼ TEASPOON BLACK PEPPER

¼ CUP CHOPPED CILANTRO

1. Place the chicken in a bowl. Add 1 tablespoon of the soy sauce, the sesame oil, and 1½ teaspoons of the cornstarch. Toss to thoroughly coat the chicken.

2. In a small bowl, combine the broth, hot pepper sauce, and the remaining 1 tablespoon soy sauce. Stir in the remaining 1½ teaspoons cornstarch until well blended.

3. In a large skillet or wok, warm 1 tablespoon of the olive oil over medium-high heat. Add the chicken and its marinade and stir-fry until the chicken is opaque but still slightly pink in the center, about 3 minutes. Transfer the chicken to a plate and cover loosely.

4. Add the remaining 1 tablespoon olive oil to the skillet. Add the scallions, celery, bell pepper, ginger, and garlic, and stir-fry until the scallions begin to wilt, about 3 minutes.

5. Return the chicken (and any juices that have collected on the plate) to the skillet and add the peanuts and black pepper. Stir the broth-cornstarch mixture and add it to the skillet. Bring the mixture to a boil and cook, stirring constantly, until the vegetables are crisp-tender and the chicken is cooked through, about 3 minutes. Stir in the cilantro and serve hot.

Oven-Baked Chicken Nuggets

SERVES 4

◆ EXTRA-QUICK

1 TO 2 GARLIC CLOVES, TO TASTE,
    PEELED

¼ CUP (PACKED) PARSLEY SPRIGS
    (OPTIONAL)

4 SLICES DAY-OLD WHOLE WHEAT OR
    WHITE BREAD, TORN INTO PIECES

¼ CUP GRATED PARMESAN CHEESE

½ TEASPOON SALT

½ TEASPOON BLACK PEPPER

2 TABLESPOONS COLD UNSALTED
    BUTTER, CUT INTO SMALL PIECES

2 TABLESPOONS MILK

1 POUND SKINLESS, BONELESS CHICKEN
    BREASTS, CUT INTO 1-INCH CUBES

1. Preheat the oven to 425°. Line a baking sheet with foil and grease it lightly.

2. Place the garlic in a food processor or blender. Process until finely chopped. Add the parsley (if using) and process until finely chopped. Add the bread, Parmesan, salt, and pepper, and process, pulsing the machine on and off, until the bread is coarsely crumbed.

3. Add the butter and process until the butter is completely incorporated. Transfer the breading to a paper or plastic bag.

4. Place the milk in a shallow bowl. Add the chicken and stir to moisten well.

5. Drain the chicken cubes in a colander, then place them in the bag of breading, and shake until well coated.

6. Place the chicken nuggets on the prepared baking sheet, leaving space between them. Bake for 12 to 15 minutes, turning the nuggets after 6 minutes, or until crisp and cooked through.

Variation: *In addition to being very popular with children, these chicken nuggets make wonderful appetizers for adults. You can leave the seasonings as they are, or add some more grown-up flavors, such as cayenne, cumin, rosemary, or curry powder. Serve the nuggets with toothpicks and a dipping sauce.*

⊙ven-Barbecued Chicken

SERVES 4

1½ TABLESPOONS OLIVE OIL
ONE 3½-POUND CHICKEN, QUARTERED
¼ CUP CIDER VINEGAR
¼ CUP KETCHUP
1 MEDIUM ONION, MINCED

2 TABLESPOONS UNSALTED BUTTER
1 TABLESPOON PAPRIKA
2 TEASPOONS LIGHT BROWN SUGAR
½ TEASPOON SALT
½ TEASPOON BLACK PEPPER

1. Preheat oven to 350°.

2. In a large nonstick skillet, warm the oil over medium heat. Add the chicken, skin-side down, and cook until lightly browned, about 10 minutes. Drain the chicken on paper towels and set aside.

3. In a medium saucepan, combine the vinegar, ketchup, onion, butter, paprika, brown sugar, salt, and pepper. Bring to a simmer over medium heat, stirring constantly. Remove the pan from the heat.

4. Transfer the chicken to a large baking dish or roasting pan, skin-side up. Pour the barbecue sauce over the chicken and cover loosely with foil. Bake for 20 minutes, basting frequently.

5. Remove the foil and increase the oven temperature to 375°. Bake for 25 minutes longer, basting frequently, or until the chicken is browned and cooked through.

6. To serve, arrange the chicken on a platter. Skim any fat from the surface of the sauce and pour the sauce over the chicken.

Variation: *Use one of the new spicy-hot ketchups in place of the regular ketchup. Or make your own salsa-style "ketchup" by straining bottled salsa to remove some of the liquid and then puréeing the solids in a blender or food processor. You may need to cook the sauce a little longer in Step 3 in order to make the mixture as thick as it would have been if you had started with bottled ketchup.*

CRISPY CHICKEN WITH HERBED BREAD CRUMBS

SERVES 4

2 GARLIC CLOVES, PEELED

4 SLICES WHITE BREAD, TORN INTO PIECES

¼ CUP GRATED ROMANO OR PARMESAN CHEESE

½ TEASPOON SALT

¼ TEASPOON BLACK PEPPER

½ TEASPOON GRATED ORANGE ZEST (OPTIONAL)

1 TEASPOON ROSEMARY OR THYME

2 TABLESPOONS COLD UNSALTED BUTTER, CUT INTO SMALL PIECES

¼ CUP BUTTERMILK OR PLAIN LOW-FAT YOGURT

PINCH OF CAYENNE PEPPER

2½ POUNDS CHICKEN PARTS

1. Preheat the oven to 375°. Line a baking sheet with foil.

2. Place the garlic in a food processor or blender. Process until finely chopped. Add the bread, Parmesan, salt, and pepper, and process, pulsing the machine on and off, until the bread is finely crumbed. Add the orange zest (if using) and rosemary, and process to distribute evenly.

3. Add the butter and process until the butter is completely incorporated. Transfer the breading to a plastic or paper bag.

4. Place the buttermilk and cayenne in a large bowl and whisk to blend. Add the chicken parts and turn to coat. Shake off any excess liquid and place the chicken, a few pieces at a time, in the bag of breading. Shake the bag until chicken is well coated.

5. Place the chicken parts on the prepared baking sheet, leaving space between them. Bake the chicken for 45 to 55 minutes, or until the coating is crisp and the juices run clear when the chicken is pierced with a knife.

ROASTED CHICKEN BREASTS WITH NEW POTATOES

SERVES 4

4 BONELESS CHICKEN BREAST HALVES,
   WITH SKIN
2 TABLESPOONS OLIVE OIL
12 SMALL RED POTATOES, HALVED
8 SHALLOTS, HALVED

½ TEASPOON SALT
½ TEASPOON BLACK PEPPER
1 TABLESPOON FLOUR
1 CUP CHICKEN BROTH, PREFERABLY
   REDUCED-SODIUM

1. Preheat the oven to 400°. Lightly oil a roasting pan large enough to hold the chicken breasts in a single layer.

2. Rub the skin side of the chicken with the oil. Place the chicken, skin-side up, in the prepared roasting pan.

3. Scatter the potatoes and shallots around the chicken and sprinkle all with the salt and pepper. Cover the pan with foil and roast for 15 minutes. Uncover the pan, baste, and roast for 20 to 30 minutes longer, or until the potatoes are tender and chicken is golden.

4. Transfer the chicken, potatoes, and shallots to a warmed serving platter. Cover the platter and keep warm in the turned-off oven with the door slightly ajar.

5. Pour off all but 2 tablespoons of the drippings from the roasting pan. Place the pan over medium-low heat and add the flour. Cook, whisking constantly, until the mixture is golden, about 3 minutes. Add the broth and continue cooking and whisking until the gravy is smooth. Reduce the heat to low and simmer for 3 to 5 minutes.

6. Drizzle half of the gravy over the chicken and potatoes, and pass the remaining gravy separately. Serve hot.

BLOODY MARY GRILLED CHICKEN

SERVES 4

1 CUP TOMATO JUICE
¼ CUP TOMATO PASTE
¼ CUP FRESH LEMON JUICE
1 TABLESPOON WORCESTERSHIRE
    SAUCE
3 DROPS HOT PEPPER SAUCE
1 TEASPOON HORSERADISH
2 GARLIC CLOVES, MINCED

1 TEASPOON SUGAR
½ TEASPOON SALT
¼ TEASPOON BLACK PEPPER
2½ POUNDS CHICKEN PARTS
2 SCALLIONS, COARSELY CHOPPED
1 FRESH PLUM TOMATO OR 1 WHOLE
    NO-SALT-ADDED CANNED TOMATO,
    COARSELY CHOPPED

1. Preheat the broiler or prepare the grill. If broiling, line a broiler pan with foil.

2. In a medium saucepan, combine the tomato juice, tomato paste, lemon juice, Worcestershire sauce, hot pepper sauce, horseradish, garlic, sugar, salt, and black pepper. Bring to a boil over medium-high heat. Reduce the heat to medium and simmer for 10 minutes, stirring occasionally. Remove the pan from the heat.

3. Place the chicken on the prepared broiler pan or the grill rack. Spoon half the tomato sauce over the chicken and broil or grill 4 inches from the heat for 12 minutes, or until the chicken begins to brown.

4. Stir the scallions and tomato into the remaining sauce in the pan.

5. Turn the chicken over and spoon the remaining sauce on the chicken. Cook 4 inches from the heat for about 12 minutes, or until the chicken is lightly browned and cooked through. Serve hot.

Chicken and Mixed Vegetable Grill

SERVES 4

5 GARLIC CLOVES, MINCED

2 SCALLIONS, COARSELY CHOPPED

¼ CUP OLIVE OIL

2 TABLESPOONS FRESH LEMON JUICE

2 TABLESPOONS GRAINY MUSTARD

3 TEASPOONS GRATED LEMON ZEST
(OPTIONAL)

1½ TEASPOONS BASIL

1½ TEASPOONS OREGANO

½ TEASPOON SALT

¼ TEASPOON BLACK PEPPER

PINCH OF CAYENNE PEPPER

4 BONE-IN CHICKEN BREAST HALVES
(ABOUT 2 POUNDS TOTAL), WITH
SKIN

1 MEDIUM ZUCCHINI, CUT INTO
½-INCH ROUNDS

1 MEDIUM YELLOW OR GREEN BELL
PEPPER, CUT INTO 1-INCH SQUARES

½ SMALL UNPEELED EGGPLANT, CUT
INTO 1-INCH CHUNKS

1. In a shallow glass or stainless steel dish, combine the garlic, scallions, oil, lemon juice, mustard, lemon zest (if using), basil, oregano, salt, black pepper, and cayenne. Mix well.

2. Add the chicken breasts and spoon the marinade over them; cover with plastic wrap and let marinate for 15 minutes.

3. Meanwhile, preheat the broiler or prepare the grill. If broiling, line a broiler pan with foil.

4. Dividing the vegetables evenly, thread the zucchini, bell pepper, and eggplant on 4 to 8 skewers.

5. Remove the chicken from the marinade, reserving the marinade. If broiling, place the chicken skin-side down on the prepared broiler pan; if grilling, place the chicken skin-side up. Broil or grill 4 inches from the heat for 7 minutes.

6. Turn the chicken over (if broiling, brush with some of the pan juices). Place the skewered vegetables on the broiler pan or grill rack and brush with the reserved marinade. Broil or grill the chicken and vegetables for 12 minutes longer, or until the chicken is cooked through. If the vegetables are done before the chicken, remove them first.

TURKEY TACO SALAD

SERVES 4

◆ EXTRA-QUICK

ONE 20-OUNCE CAN RED KIDNEY
  BEANS, RINSED AND DRAINED
ONE 16-OUNCE CAN NO-SALT-ADDED
  CORN KERNELS
⅔ CUP MILD SALSA
½ CUP REDUCED-FAT SOUR CREAM
1 TABLESPOON CUMIN
½ TEASPOON SALT

½ TEASPOON BLACK PEPPER
½ POUND ROAST TURKEY, CUT INTO
  ½-INCH CUBES
3 CELERY RIBS, DICED
8 ROMAINE LETTUCE LEAVES,
  SHREDDED
2 CUPS TORTILLA CHIPS

1. Place the kidney beans and corn in a strainer or colander and set them aside to drain thoroughly.

2. Meanwhile, in a small bowl, stir together the salsa, sour cream, cumin, salt, and pepper.

3. In a large bowl, combine the beans, corn, turkey, and celery, and toss to combine. Add the dressing and toss.

4. Divide the lettuce among 4 salad plates and spoon the turkey salad on top. Garnish each serving with some tortilla chips, whole or crumbled.

SWEET AFTERTHOUGHT: *Toss chunks of pineapple (fresh or canned) and banana with some lemon juice to keep the banana from discoloring. Just before serving, sprinkle the fruit with toasted coconut and brown sugar (or granulated maple sugar) to taste.*

INDEX

Recipes that are marked in the body of the book with the symbol ◆ take 30 minutes or less to prepare. They are grouped in the index under the name Extra-Quick. Recipes that are marked in the body of the book with the symbol ◇ derive 30% or fewer of their calories from fat. They are grouped in the index under the name Low-Fat.